sands press

NIGHT WITCHES

MIRREN HOGAN

sands press

sands press

A division of 3244601 Canada Inc.
300 Central Avenue West
Brockville, Ontario
K6V 6K8

Toll Free 1-800-563-0911 or 613-345-2687
http://www.sandspress.com

ISBN 978-1-988281-16-2

Cover concept and artwork by Craig O'Neill
Formatting by Kevin Davidson & Renee Hare
Publisher Sands Press

1st Printing March 2017

To book an author for your live event, please call: 1-800-563-0911

Sands Press is a literary publisher interested in new and established authors wishing to develop and market their product.

For more information please visit our website at www.sandspress.com.

PROLOGUE

It was early in the day, but I was already tired. At my age, that was to be expected. I looked across my small sitting room at the journalist. I already couldn't remember the name of the American newspaper she worked for, but I could recall the past as though it had just happened, like I was still young and strong.

"When Germany invaded the Soviet Union on June 22nd, 1941, I couldn't believe it," I said. "I sat by the radio with my mother on that first morning. We listened to the news and hoped it wasn't true. My country had signed a non-aggression pact with Germany to avoid this very thing." To this day, it shamed me that we had been allies with the Nazis for a time.

"As you probably know, reports of German spies and incursions had been coming in for weeks, but had been dismissed. We ordinary people didn't know any of that, so the invasion came as a great shock. I remember my mother looking pale, on the verge of tears." I could still picture her face, although the memory was more vague with each passing year.

"It was as though she knew this was a pivotal moment for us all. Operation Barbarossa, they called it. Over three million German troops suddenly thrown at us." I spoke softly, the moment still held in my mind's eye. "We went from having normal lives, to being at war, from one day to the next. For a while, war still seemed like a distant thing rather than something that was actually taking place a few hundred kilometres away. As days passed, we saw more and more young men, all in various uniforms — heading off in trucks and trains — for the front line. All the soldiers, the snipers, the aviators; we lost so many, especially in those early days. Millions of men and boys. Such a waste." I shook my head.

"My mother and I became obsessed with listening to the radio, hearing reports of the German push toward Leningrad and Minsk. Of course Leningrad is St Petersburg now." Sometimes I caught myself thinking of them by their old names, now changed because of their significance to the former communist

1

regime.

The reporter nodded and made a note on her tablet. Modern technology never failed to baffle me. I still preferred paper and pencil. How times change. I guess this is what we fought for, to make things better for the next generation.

"Food started to run low. We struggled to make everything last a little bit longer. Day by day, the Germans seemed to be getting closer. They took Smolensk, to the west of Moscow, after two long bloody months of fighting. It seemed inevitable they'd eventually come here." I shivered, reliving the growing feeling of fear from those days.

"But of course, I didn't just sit idly by and wait for the Germans to come. Oh no, us Russian women are made from sterner stuff." I drew myself up proudly.

"What did you do?" the reporter asked, her hand poised over her tablet. I hadn't had such an enraptured audience in many years. It was gratifying to know after all this time, people were still interested in the things I'd seen and done. This wouldn't be easy, but I wanted to have my say at last.

"I'll get us coffee," I said, rising unsteadily to my feet. "Then I will tell you my story."

CHAPTER 1

I brushed the hair out of my face with the back of my hand and listened to the distant explosions. The acrid smell of gunpowder laced the insides of my nostrils. It was all I could smell, all I'd been able to smell for days. That and smoke pluming from burning roofs, set on fire by the German bombs. No one slept. The noise and fear kept us awake; the crying of children and screams of the wounded, the tanks rumbling closer, our own jangled nerves.

I bent to jam the shovel into the autumn mud. My shoulders and back ached, but when I wanted to give up, I worked faster, dug deeper. I had the blood of workers in my veins, and we worked while we still had strength to stand. Men were dying. A few aches, a blister or two and bleeding skin were all nothing. Stopping even for a little while might be all the enemy needed.

I had only seen a tank from a distance; the solid outer shell and massive gun like a giant eye. It was a thing to be feared, a harbinger of our death. I visualized, in my mind, an enemy tank trying to roll over the ditch we were digging. Instead of moving on, it would slide inside, its treads stuck irreversibly, churning fruitlessly, until Russian soldiers came along to kill the men inside. The thought filled me with such a savage delight that I surprised myself with the viciousness of the thought. For a moment, the poor mud became the head of the enemy, yielding under my cold steel.

"You're going to hurt yourself," the woman beside me remarked, smiling at me over a shovel that looked too long and heavy for her to handle.

I frowned at her at first, mistrusting her motive for speaking words like that to me. I hated the thought that anyone would think me weak. But then I smiled.

"It's not myself I want to hurt, " I said. "I'd like to use this to kill a few Nazis." I raised my shovel and wielded it like a club. "Since they won't give us guns."

"What would you do with a gun?" she asked, laughing at me and my fierce stance. "Don't you know, war isn't women's business." She said the words as though she were quoting and rolled her eyes skyward. Her mouth became a smirk of derision. I knew she'd either read them or been told them, but didn't believe them herself, any more than I did.

"My city is my business, as it is yours," I replied firmly. I lowered my shovel quickly and went back to digging. "Our motherland is my business." Since childhood, I had been aware of the importance of my home, like all Russian children, but war has a way of making us see and value what we have even more. It makes us want to stand up and defend every blade of glass; every last bit of dirt; every drop of water or blood. And more, we may not have a perfect way of life, but we would defend our right to live it to the death.

The young woman, she wasn't much older than I was, nodded and smiled again. "I wanted to be a sniper, but they wouldn't take me. Maybe now they will." She nodded in the direction of the advancing German army.

My eyes widened. A sniper? Would she even be as tall as the rifle?

She took in my expression and laughed again. "What? You don't think I can shoot? My father taught me. He was a sniper in the Civil War. And this one too, until he was killed. A plane strafed his unit." Her expression clouded and for a moment I thought she might cry. She didn't though; she bit her lip and drew in a loud breath, then exhaled mist into the cold afternoon.

I nodded. There wasn't a person amongst us who hadn't lost people they knew or loved.

"I had two brothers. One was killed on the first day, the day the Germans invaded. My other brother is missing. I think he might be dead too." I felt treacherous voicing that fear out loud. Until now, I hadn't. My mother would have scolded me for saying it. She'd have shaken her wooden spoon at me. The woman would cling to the hope he'd return home until she knew for certain that he wouldn't. My mother's tenacity was matched for size only by her big heart and generous hips, slimmed down now from months on increasingly meagre rations. She didn't want to think he was dead. Neither did I.

"My mother is in the city," I jerked my head back toward it. My father, I would not discuss. I still had nightmares occasionally about him being arrested and taken away. We had no word from or about him for weeks afterward, but I'll never forget my mother's anguished face when a government official had told her he'd been executed as an enemy of the state. That was three years ago. I loved

4

him, but we lived with the same shame every day, even though none of us knew what he'd actually done.

"She refuses to leave." I muttered something about stubborn people, but I didn't blame her. I had also refused to leave. How could I go when I could be of use? The Germans would learn; we Russians don't give up so easily.

"And here we are, digging ditches when there are Nazis to be killed," she leaned down to pick up a rock and tossed it aside. "I think, when I'm done here, I'll go and ask again and not leave until I'm accepted." She wiped mud from her hand onto her trousers and squinted at me.

"What about you?" she asked. "What would you do, if they let you?"

Hours and hours of digging had given me a lot of time to think about that. So much time that I'd gone over and over the question in my head, mulling the various options that made up the Soviet war machine, and coming up with a conclusion.

"I want to fly," I declared. I had asked when the Germans first violated us by invading our motherland. I had gone straight down to the recruitment office and I stood in line and waited. I was the only woman in the line and I waited for hours, while the line moved as slowly as a stream in winter. I hadn't cared. I'd have waited for days, if it meant defending my homeland.

Eventually, it had been my turn to speak to the recruitment officers. They had looked me up and down, and one gave in to a thinly veiled attempt not to laugh.

"What are you doing here, little girl?" The other one asked, his brown eyes looking derisively at me. He had a cranky face, a bulbous nose, and I was not a little girl. I was twenty years old. I knew I would only get off on the wrong foot if I pointed that out to them, so I decided on politeness.

"I want to join the PVO or VVS." Both were aerial defence forces and either were my first choice, but really, I'd have done anything that was asked of me, as long as I got to the front to fight.

The laughing man laughed even harder. I couldn't stop myself from giving him a scowl. The fascists were not only on our doorstep but had crossed over the threshold and this man could only laugh as though I'd told some great joke.

"Go home, we don't need the help of girls." The cranky-faced man glared at me, as if appalled that I dared to ask. Then he was the first to tell me those words, "War is not the business of women."

"If it is not the business of people to fight for their motherland, then whose is it?" I argued, but they'd stopped listening. I'd found myself pushed aside and back out onto the street. The line was longer now, men, men and more men, and boys, all willing to die for Russia. I should have applauded them, but instead, I trudged off in humiliation.

That was June, now it was October and the war wasn't going well for us. I'd left college, where I had been studying to be a teacher and waited, as everyone else had, for the victory that hadn't come, or to help when needed. The Germans kept on winning and we kept on losing and now they were all but at our gates.

"I want to fly, I want to bomb the fascists and shoot down their planes before they can bomb our cities and towns." I knew I sounded dogmatic, but I prefer to think of it as passionate. In spite of that, I half expected the woman to laugh, as the man at the recruitment centre had laughed. Instead, she nodded.

"Why don't you then?" she asked, as if the answer was so obvious. She must have noticed my look of confusion, because a smile broke out on her face and I knew she was about to say something I'd like to hear.

"You haven't heard? Marina Raskova herself has asked for volunteer recruits to join a women's regiment."

My heart skipped a beat, maybe several. I hardly dared to breathe, in case she told me she was joking. Marina Mikhailovna Raskova was a hero of mine, of many women. She'd already been awarded a gold star, a Hero of the Soviet Union medal for her accomplishments before the war. Her flight with Ospienko and Grizodubova in the Rodina was the stuff of legends. The three aviators had set out to break a record in 1938. Their plane had crashed, but Raskova had bailed out first. She'd parachuted into a swamp and had walked for ten days, hungry, tired, with injured legs, and alone to find her plane.

Every young woman, and many older ones, idolised her. If she were organising regiments of airwomen, then women would come. I would go; I'd apply right away.

A distant explosion rudely reminded me of where I was and what I was supposed to be doing. The cold shovel in my hand, precious dirt under my feet. I would dig this ditch and then I'd go and sign up. I'd defend the soil beneath my feet and the people who walked upon it.

*****

I washed and changed into my best dress, one made of simple blue wool that fell past my knees, and my nicest leather shoes. Neither was anything grand, but I wouldn't embarrass myself or my family. I might have wanted to fight and maybe kill, but I was still a young woman, with some small measure of vanity left.

I brushed my long dark hair and tied it back off my face. Glancing in the mirror I practiced my stern expression in the old, mottled glass. The man in the recruitment office had had a stern expression on his face when he'd told me 'no'. I wanted to have one as well so they knew I wouldn't listen to another refusal. I smiled at myself, seeing a young woman in the mirror, but one who wouldn't be pushed aside quite so easily this time.

I marched out the door and onto the street. It was getting quieter in Moscow as the days went on. The feeling of fear and desperation rose with the scent of gunpowder. It was getting dark too, every night passed in blackout. We hoped to thwart enemy bombs by making fewer targets for them to see.

I scanned the sky, but only saw wafting smoke. Perhaps we'd be lucky tonight and they wouldn't come. Of course, they probably would. I sighed heavily, making an old man turn and look at me as he walked by. Rather than thinking me odd, he nodded his understanding and shuffled on his way. Of course, war has a way of binding people together, giving us a single purpose, a common enemy.

The sky was golden and red by the time I reached the recruitment office. War was hell, but it made for pretty twilights and sunsets. I decided there must be some meaning to it, some sort of indication I'd succeed. I'm not usually superstitious, but I could use all the confidence I could get.

The line was much smaller now than it had been in the early days of the war. Anyone who had been allowed to fight had gone, apart from a few who had been too old or perhaps too young and hadn't succeeded in lying about their age, and women, like me. The laughing man and Cranky-face were gone. In their place was a man with only one arm and a haunted expression in his grey-blue eyes. His face and posture spoke of a man who had been to the front, and had returned, but just barely, and who now spent his days sending others to the front in his place.

"Good afternoon," he greeted me with a weary tone.

I'd thought about what I wanted to say over and over on the walk here. How I'd be insistent and firm. But it when it came time to speak, the words I'd rehearsed just didn't seem right.

"I would like to apply to join Marina Raskova's regiment," I replied, simple and to the point. I waited for him to laugh, but he didn't. Instead, he grabbed a sheet of paper and slid it over the tabletop to me. His hand was scarred, the tips of two long fingers were missing. He was probably grateful he had a hand left at all, even damaged as it was. I had seen a few people return from the fighting, but not this close up. It should probably have scared me, but it made me more resolute. Why should anyone sit back and watch while the Germans were doing this to our people?

"You're the fifth one today," he told me. I thought he was going to smile, but he didn't do that either. He handed me a pen and a small bottle of ink. "Fill that out and I'll send it off."

Surprised into silence, I nodded and hurriedly wrote, dipping the nib into the ink every few seconds. My name, Nadia Valinsky; my address; my qualifications; the names of my mother and brothers (in case any were also considered enemies of the state). I picked up the sheet, held it pinched between my thumbs and forefingers and waved it to dry the ink. Even a tiny smudge might render it unreadable enough to disqualify me.

Satisfied, I handed the paper back to the man. He glanced at it and nodded, then placed it at the top of a neat pile and turned to the person next in line behind me. The dismissal this time was as sudden as the first, but a little more positive. It wasn't a 'no' this time, just a 'wait and see.'

CHAPTER 2

Somehow I managed to sleep. The bombs were blasting another part of the city tonight. Perhaps they were outside the city. Either way, they were distant, intermittently disturbing my turbulent thoughts. Mostly, I heard silence, as though the city was collectively holding its breath, waiting. When I slept, I dreamed of flying, soaring over Moscow on my own wings, tossing bombs onto men in strange uniforms, watching them being blasted apart.

It wasn't surprising then that I awoke sweating and flailing. The blankets were sideways on my bed, and hanging half off. My mother was standing over me, one hand shaking me.

"Nadia, are you going to sleep all day?" No one ever accused my mother of either wasting words or affection. Her sons, she adored. Me, she tolerated.

"Get married," she'd say. "Have babies."

"To who?" I argued back. "All the good men are at the front, or dead." Of course I'd regret the words as soon as I'd said them, because I'd reminded her of my brother. She'd pull out her handkerchief and wipe her eyes, ignoring me while I tried to apologize. No matter what I did, I ended up always being the one begging forgiveness.

"Wake up, this is for you." I realized she had a telegram in her hand. She tossed it onto the top of my quilt and left the room.

I sat up and unfolded the telegram. The note was from Major Raskova, of all people. It simply said, "Come for an interview, pack well. You may not be returning home." She didn't waste words, either. For a moment I was scared she might turn out to be a younger version of my mother, but when Marina Raskova told me to go, I would go, and go gladly.

I only had a battered old suitcase, but I swung it onto my bed and started packing my nicest dresses and shoes. I didn't want to look bad in front of Major Raskova. It was important to me that she see me as a competent, presentable young woman. I had hardly worn the white cotton dress my father had bought for me, I may not even fit into it anymore, but I tossed it into my case on top of the rest.

My mother came back into the room and frowned at me. I held my breath as she looked down at the telegram. She picked it up and read it. I held my breath and stood ready to hold my ground. No matter what she said, I was going. This was something I wanted to do — needed to do — something my motherland needed me to do.

My mother looked from the telegram to my suitcase. "Silly girl," she scolded. "Are you going to a dance?" She grabbed my suitcase, tipped it upside down and emptied it onto my bed. "It's October. You need warm things." She grabbed my trousers and warm coat from my tiny, rickety cupboard and started re-packing for me, folding everything neatly before closing and clicking my suitcase shut. I simply stood back and watched in silence, too surprised to speak.

I'd seen her cry once, over my older brother, but never over me, until now. She didn't weep, thankfully, but her eyes were shining and a tear trickled over her short lashes. It was strange and a little disconcerting. She was the rock of the family; the idea she'd lose her composure for my sake shook me.

"I've lost a husband and then two children to this war," she said brokenly, "You come home." She looked at me and nodded curtly. "You must come home."

That was an order I intended to obey.

That was the first time I ever heard her admit that my younger brother might be dead and it almost brought me to tears.

"I will, Mother," I went to embrace her and found myself caught in a warm hug, her arms holding me hard to her until I almost couldn't breathe. "I promise."

"My Konfetka," she stroked my hair softly. She hadn't called me sweetie since I was a child. If anything would help me to come home, it was knowing my mother loved me and would miss me after all.

"Ya tebya lyublyu," she told me, pulling away finally and looking in my eyes.

"I love you too, Mother." I bent to pick up my suitcase and kissed her cheek. It was only an interview. I might be back in a few hours. Or I might never return.

*****

The Zhukovsky Air Force Engineering Academy building was large, cream coloured and filled with women. There were so many of us, we spilled out into the corridor. Some sat, some stood, some were calm and some, like me, looked as though they couldn't keep still. More than one was biting her nails or pacing restlessly. I took my place at the end of the long queue, my suitcase at my feet.

"Have you ever seen so many girls in one place?" The woman beside me tried to whisper, but her voice carried over quite a distance. She was tall, taller than me. She was probably taller than everyone else here as well. Her build was solid, but with curves and a mass of curly, blonde hair. She might never be beautiful, but her nervous smile made me like her right away.

"I don't think I have," I replied, giving her a nervous smile back. "I'm Nadia. Do you think all of these women want to join the regiment?"

"Sophia Alanina, and I heard three regiments," she told me. "I think they're looking for more than pilots. They need navigators, mechanics and all of that."

I nodded slowly. "There are still too many of us for that." A regiment might consist of a hundred or so people, including all of the ground crews and administration staff. "Even if they make three regiments, there has to be more that twice that number of women here. They won't take us all." There were only so many aircraft and only so much space to train us all.

Sophia nodded grimly and shuffled forward as the line moved. Her eyes fixed on something. A tall, severe-looking woman was waving girls forward, two at a time, through a doorway at the far end of the corridor. Every time the door opened, everyone would stop and watch.

"Oh, it looks like she's going home," Sophia whispered as two women exited, one looking thrilled, the other despondent. We watched the despondent woman, her shoulders slumped, heading out the door, lugging a heavy-looking bag. As much as I felt sorry for her, I hoped that wouldn't be me. I drew myself up a little straighter, a subconscious act to make me feel more suitable, even though I knew it'd change nothing.

"They only want the best," I said softly.

"Of course they do," a small, dark- haired woman on the other side of Sophia spoke up. "Look at all of these women. More than half will be sent home. Just in time to evacuate." She looked appraisingly at us both and from the disdain in her eyes, she didn't much care for what she saw. The feeling was immediately mutual. It wasn't usually like me to take an instant dislike to anyone, but as she seemed to have made her mind up quickly enough, I couldn't help but respond in kind. It was unlikely to matter one way or another, as after today, I might never see her again.

"We'll have to evacuate if we get chosen anyway, Lena," Sophia said evenly, "They're not going to train us here in Moscow."

"Us?" Lena asked. "How many flying hours do you have?"

"Not as many as you," Sophia conceded, "but I'd bet it's more than some of the girls here."

My heart sank. Maybe I didn't have enough hours either. I had spent the last couple of years studying at the university and flying after class. I had at least a hundred hours of flying time. Some of these women would probably have many times that.

I looked down at my old leather suitcase and pictured myself lugging it all the way home. Then what would I do? Maybe I'd go and train to be a sniper. How difficult could shooting a gun really be?

"Besides," Sophia went on, "they might need someone to pull aircraft off the runway after you crash it."

Lena gave her a filthy look and might have responded but she, and a curly haired woman a little older than me, were waved forward. Sophia and I would be next.

"Don't worry about her," Sophia reassured me as the door closed and Lena couldn't hear us. "Lena Turova is all talk. She's an excellent pilot; the problem is that she knows it. She thinks she's the next Marina Raskova, or better maybe." She sighed. "Perhaps she is," she admitted. "She's sure to be chosen as a pilot."

I grimaced uncharitably, not liking myself for doing it. "Well if they need the best," I reasoned, "then I suppose she should be." The thought of her killing Germans while I hid in a bomb shelter, dug ditches or evacuated to I-didn't-know-where was something I didn't want to consider. "Did she really crash a plane?"

"Only once, but she hates being reminded," Sophia grinned. "It doesn't make her less of a pilot. Or better than all of us," she added hastily.

"We have to be chosen," I said forcefully. I glanced over my shoulder as the woman behind me raised an eyebrow at me. She was blonde, like Sophia, but so light that I doubted it was natural. She was also tiny, at least a head shorter than me. I had no idea how she'd see out of a cockpit, but she had an intense look in her eyes that might make the whole German army tremble. She was also immaculately dressed. I have no idea how she managed that, during a war.

I smiled at her. She smiled back, but it was a distracted one, as though she was focused on something else entirely.

"Nadia," I gestured toward myself.

"Hmm? Oh, Lillya." She nodded and then turned away, not rudely, simply

12

preoccupied.

I glanced back at Sophia, who shrugged. "War brings all sorts of people together," she said softly. That was obvious. I looked to the interview room door and wondered what was going on inside.

I didn't have to wait long. It swung open and Lena Turova, looking very pleased with herself, all but swaggered out. She smiled at Sophia and I.

"I'd wish you luck, but..." She shrugged and walked off, the same direction the other successful applicants had gone.

"What was that supposed to mean?" I whispered, leaning down to pick up my suitcase.

"Like I said, she's all talk. She's probably just trying to put us off. I went to the same aviation school and she was like this the entire time." And yet, Sophia sounded rattled. I knew I was. My heart was racing, my palms were sweaty and I felt as though I'd trip over my own tongue. I had to be accepted, if only to prove Lena Turova wrong.

Together, we walked through the doorway and Sophia closed the door behind us. I put down my suitcase and looked over to the desk. My nerves, already bad enough, suddenly felt a thousand times worse. The butterflies in my stomach became birds with the wingspan of an albatross. I was glad I hadn't eaten today, because I might have thrown it up all over the floor.

There, sitting behind the desk, was Marina Raskova herself. Her dark brown hair was parted in the centre and tied back in a bun at the nape of her neck. Not too many people would have gotten away with such a severe look, but on her it was fitting. Hers were the bluest eyes I'd ever seen, staring back at me. She looked a little tired, but I was no less in awe.

I glanced at Sophia out of the corner of my eye and tried not to smile, seeing her standing in the same pose I'd automatically adopted; back straight, hands folded over each other in front of us. I swallowed and focused all of my attention on the woman behind the desk.

"Your names please?" she asked, her voice soft, almost musical. I knew she'd had training as a singer in her childhood. It was obvious she'd been taught to make the most of her voice.

"Nadia Valinsky." Somehow I managed to speak without mumbling or becoming tongue-tied.

"Sophia Alanina."

Raskova nodded to us both. I wouldn't have been surprised if she remembered our names later.

"You understand what I'm asking for are women to go into battle?" she asked.

I nodded. Before I could reply, she spoke again.

"Some of those women will not return." She looked from one of us to the other and back again, her tone never changing. Her words were harsh, but I knew that must have been her intention. "Some will die, or lose a leg or an arm or a hand. Or both. You understand this?"

I remembered the man in the recruitment office and nodded. "Yes, Major Raskova." It was peculiar to refer to a woman by military rank, but it suited her.

She sat forward in her chair and focused her blue eyes directly on my face. "You understand you may die?"

"Yes, ma'am." I was less confident now. Was she trying to talk me out of it? I was determined not to be so easily deterred. I hadn't waited so long only to back out after a few well-chosen words.

She regarded me for a moment and then sat back in her chair. "What is it that you want to do?" she asked kindly.

"Fly." Sophia and I spoke in unison. That earned us the faintest of smiles from our idol.

"You were in college?" she asked me, looking down at a sheet of paper. I recognised my writing on the application.

"Yes, ma'am." I wasn't sure what the relevance was. Perhaps she thought I wasn't dedicated enough to my flight training and practice.

"I need both of you in my regiments," Raskova said, looking back up. "Sophia, you will be an armourer." Somehow that didn't surprise me. Sophia was hefty and strong. She'd do better at lifting bombs than a lot of us. Not that I wouldn't do my best if that's what I was chosen for, but I was desperate to pilot the aircraft that dropped the bombs.

"Nadia."

When Raskova spoke my name, I realised I was holding my breath. I was going to fly. I was going to the front, to defend my country. I was…

"You will be a navigator."

My heart sank and I know my expression went with it. A navigator? I looked at Raskova's face and knew there was no point in arguing. At best, I knew she wouldn't hear it. At worst, she might send me home. That she had started out as a navigator buoyed my spirits somewhat and gave me courage to reply. "Yes,

Major Raskova."

"Good. Please go to the room at the end of the corridor with the other women. From there, you'll get your sleeping arrangements. You'll all be staying together tonight. We leave Moscow in a few days. Thank you."

That was my third but best dismissal since the war had begun. I was in. I was going to the front. Sophia and I made a dignified exit, started up the corridor and then looked at each other and shared a warm embrace, as though we were already sisters.

We were going to the front.

CHAPTER 3

I don't think anyone got much sleep that night; I know I didn't. Packed into small rooms with as many other women as would fit, we talked and laughed and sang all night. Many of us separated into groups; the pilots in one, navigators in another, armorers and mechanics in their own. Whether that was by choice or design, I didn't know. That didn't mean we didn't mingle, we did. I spent most of the night beside Sophia and avoiding Lena Turova. That was easy enough; the other woman made herself scarce early in the night, her time spent only in the company of other pilots.

The small blonde woman told us her name was Lydia Litviak, although she pointed out, "I prefer Lillya. Or Lil'ka. Anything but Lydia." I thought Lydia was a pretty name, but we were all soon calling her Lillya. We gigged as she told us she needed to have the pedals adjusted on the planes she flew because she was too short to reach.

"They have to put blocks on them to make them higher. Occasionally I remember to take them off for the next pilot." She smiled so sweetly that for a moment I believed she really did mean to remove them. But then I saw the glint of mischief in her grey-blue eyes and laughed.

"You're terrible," I told her.

"Oh no, not I." She gave me a look of such sweet contrition that I almost felt bad for saying it, until I realised she was acting. That look must have let her get away with a lot that she probably shouldn't have, but I liked her tenacity. I stuck my tongue out at her and she dissolved into giggles. Sometimes she was so intense that it was nice to see that she was just a girl like the rest of us.

"Do you know, 'Po ulitse mastavoi shla dyevitsa'?" Sophia asked. We burst into a chorus of 'Along the paved road there went a girl…', singing as loudly as we could.

I don't know what time it was when an older sergeant stuck his head into our rooms, looking stern and frowning at us.

"Are you girls air force or canaries?" he asked. We howled with laughter. For a moment I thought he'd be cranky and maybe order Major Raskova to send us home, but he shook his head and smiled like someone's indulgent uncle. He left, closing the door behind him and we sang a little louder, just for him.

Not long after that, we did lie down and try to sleep, but excited whispers passed back and forth through the rooms. No one got more than a few minutes of quiet at a time until a couple of hours before dawn, when everyone eventually fell into an exhausted sleep.

Of course, we were woken at dawn for a quick breakfast and to be told our uniforms had arrived.

"Funny," I remarked to Sophia, "I hadn't thought about uniforms before." Of course we can't just have been recruited and then sent off to fight. Obviously, since none of us yet knew how to shoot or drop bombs on targets from aircraft. "I hadn't thought beyond being accepted," I admitted.

"Of course not, no one did. You're all lucky to get this far," Lena told me, from across the long, ancient table around which some of us were seated. Even though she was correct, I couldn't help but think she was making it a personal insult toward me. Being spoken to like that, in front of so many others, was slightly humiliating and it irked me so much I couldn't keep myself from responding.

"As are you. After all, not long ago they weren't accepting women at all," I said.

I glared at Lena and sipped my weak, warm tea. It wasn't great, but it was the first I'd had in months and was sufficient to gag myself with before I spoke out further.

"We all are lucky," Sophia added, nodding her agreement.

Lena tilted her head to regard Sophia, an unpleasant expression on her otherwise pretty face. "And what are you, exactly? What job were you chosen for?" She sounded very much as though she didn't think Sophia should be there at all, which would have been a grave insult to the judgement of Major Raskova.

"I'm an armourer," Sophia replied proudly, her shoulders drawn up and squared. "I'll be the one loading bombs onto your plane so you can blow up fascists."

"Oh yes," Lena replied, as if somehow this explained everything.

Considering the armourers were the strongest and often the tallest of us, and would know what to do with large, dangerous explosives, I thought Lena would be either brave or foolish if she insulted them.

"Yes," Sophia replied cheerfully. "Luckily you don't need brains to kill people." Somehow she made a self-deprecating remark sound like an insult. Obviously Lena thought so too, because she gave Sophia the filthiest look.

"It helps," the woman next to Lena pointed out. "But the most educated are the navigators. You had better be nice to them, because they can get you lost." She winked at me and I smiled back.

Lena made a rude noise and turned her face away. Before she did, I saw a flash of something in her eyes and recognized fear. What was she scared of and why she was taking it out on us, I could only guess, but hopefully she'd get over it. An attitude like hers could get her and her wing mates killed. With a shrug in Sophia's direction, I finished my breakfast and we all headed off to get our uniforms.

"Oh my."

We jostled and shuffled into a small room, the original use of which I could only speculate. Tables set to each side were obscured by piles of uniforms. They were stacked neatly, but there was so much of everything. Trousers to one side, shirts to another, coats beside them and boots, lots of boots. It was all but a sea of brownish green; drab but functional. From the laundered smell intermingled with the faintest traces of embedded sweat, they weren't new. I, for one, had no desire to learn where they had come from.

"Well what did you expect, a fashion parade?" I heard someone whisper to the girl beside her.

At the doorway was the sergeant-uncle from the night before, his arms crossed over a broad chest. He might have been handsome once, in his youth, but he was old now, at least forty. His hair was receding from his forehead and he had lines around his eyes, but they were still a bright, laughing blue.

"Here you are, canaries. We spared some uniforms for you. You'll have to look through them and pick out your own. We don't have time to sort them out for you." Although his words were harsh, his tone was kind and, I think, amused, or maybe just tolerant. Taking care of a group of would-be warrior women was evidently a novelty. Hopefully we could prove we were worthy of being taken seriously.

"Well," the woman who had championed navigators at breakfast spoke up, her hands planted on her hips, "if you don't have time to sort them, then you don't have time to stand there and watch us change." She shooed him out the door, helped by Sophia and a few other girls. He was shaking his head and smiling, but he went. The door was closed firmly and we dove into the piles of clothes.

We quickly discovered there was nothing fashionable about our uniforms; nothing feminine, either. In fact, they'd sent us men's uniforms and everything was too big.

I managed to get over to the pile of shirts and picked up the first one on the top of the pile. It looked a little big but I shrugged into it and started doing up the buttons. The sleeves hung past my hands so far that they disappeared under the cuffs. I stepped back from the piles to let others in while I rolled up the sleeves. The hem was too long, but I could tuck that into my trousers, assuming I could find some that fit. I turned to the woman beside me and smiled.

"Maybe I could just put a belt around my waist and wear it as a dress."

She giggled and waved her arms up and down, her sleeves flapping over her hands. "I think I need to cut some sleeve off."

I smiled and looked over to the pile of trousers on the other side of the room. I started working my way through the press of giggling women, stepping over discarded items as I went. I didn't get very far before I heard Sophia call my name.

"Nadia! Catch!"

Instinctively I raised my hands and caught the pair of trousers she'd tossed to me. Grinning, I held them up against myself. They were far too long. They'd swallow my feet and my boots. I rolled them up and threw them back, roughly in her direction. My aim was terrible; the trousers hit a tall, dark-haired girl and slid to the floor. She turned and laughed, before picking them up and placing them back on the table.

It took me several minutes, but I managed to reach the pile and snagged a second pair. They were even longer than the first, and wide enough to fit two of me inside.

Resigned, I put them aside and picked up another pair before someone else did. I pulled them on over my own trousers and leaned down to roll up the hems. They were so big the crotch hung down to my knees. I grabbed a hold of the fabric at the front and pulled them up, but I knew I couldn't stay like that for long.

I felt ridiculous until I looked up and saw all of the other girls were having the same problem. Everyone was wearing an oversized shirt, and trousers that looked like mine. Many were waddling around like ducks, struggling to walk in the excess of fabric. There, in the centre of the room, stood tiny Lillya Litviak, wearing a huge shirt, enormous trousers, a coat that hung to the floor and boots that made her look like a child in her father's footwear. She was smiling, looking like a queen as if nothing was amiss and I couldn't help but laugh; she looked so comical.

Everyone else was laughing as well, at themselves and at everyone else. Shirts and trousers were being tossed across the room, back and forth to girls who couldn't reach the right piles. It was starting to look as though a bomb had gone off in here, scattering garments in its blast.

A coat was thrown and I managed to catch it. Of course it didn't fit, but in the deep of winter I might not mind that I could tuck my fingers up inside the sleeves. It was also long enough that I could probably use it as a blanket if I needed to. I had a feeling I'd be grateful for both someday.

And then there were the boots. I hadn't realised men had such big feet. I could have fit one and a half of mine into the boots I grabbed. I leaned against a wall, pressed my feet down into them and tried to walk. Rather than the dignified stroll I might have hoped for, I shuffled along like a penguin. I hoped that no one was expecting us to march anywhere in them.

Wiping tears of laughter out of the corners of my eyes, I looked around for Sophia.

"Personally, I don't see what the problem is," she was saying.

"Of course you don't, you fit into yours!" I cried out in response.

The clothes might not have fit her curves, but she didn't have to roll up a hem or a sleeve. For some reason, that made me laugh even harder than before. Her boots were still too big, but she'd at least walk with more dignity than the rest of us.

I scanned the room, looking at the faces of the women around me. Somehow, I sensed moments like these, when we could be carefree, would be few from now until the war ended. At least we looked the part, more or less, although I wasn't sure how far I'd get in my boots until I stuffed them to fill the extra room inside them. Perhaps the dress I'd snuck into my suitcase when my mother wasn't looking would come in useful for that.

"At this rate, we won't need bombs or grenades," someone commented. "The Germans would laugh themselves to death." For a moment, her words were greeted by silence. Then we all howled with laughter, and kept laughing until our sides ached and the sergeant-uncle came to find us, to make sure we were still quite sane.

CHAPTER 4

I stamped my feet in my oversized boots and tucked my hands up deeper under my arms. The October night was bitterly cold. The air smelled like sleet, or maybe snow. My numb toes made me wish I were tucked into my nice warm bed. A scarf wound twice around my neck also covered my mouth and my sleeves covered my hands past my fingertips, but I was still freezing. This winter was going to be particularly merciless.

The train station was crowded, both with Raskova's regiments and desperate Muscovite evacuees. Men, women and children had amassed in the sub-zero temperatures, all hoping to flee Moscow before the Germany army arrived in force and took the city. It would be days, maybe less, from what we'd heard. The feeling of fear and the smell of gunpowder increased almost hourly. The enemy would want to beat us before the snow settled in and they all froze to death. We would hold them off and hope they did freeze.

I glanced at Sophia. Her face was pink, but otherwise she didn't look as cold as I felt. I didn't know how she did it. Some of the other women were shivering, their teeth chattering audibly. Caught in the light of someone's hand-held torch, their breath filled the air with mist, like smoke, which hung in the air for several moments before evaporating. And yet, no one complained, at least not out loud.

"Have you got any idea where are we going?" I whispered, looking up at Sophia briefly before turning my eyes back toward Major Raskova.

She was talking to a man on the opposite side of the station and gesturing with her gloved hands. The man nodded and pointed toward an idling train. He was speaking rapidly, but I couldn't hear him over the station noise.

"I don't know, but I think we're going soon," Sophia said, hefting her bag higher onto her shoulder. We'd been waiting in Moscow for four days, getting anxious, excited and restless, while the evacuees poured out of the city. Going back to digging anti-tank ditches would have helped to work off the nervous energy, but the chance was denied us. The Air Force was keeping us all close.

"This is us," Inna Markova, the woman beside me, commented. She nodded toward Major Raskova, whose deliberate steps would bring her to the front of the group of women. I wondered if I could ever be so poised. Even without speaking, she commanded the attention of every woman in the regiment. What had been nervous chatter immediately died down to a deferential silence.

Speaking low, but loud enough for even those at the back to hear, she said, "This is our train. Please board in the following order and be seated; pilots first, then navigators, mechanics, and finally armourers." She always referred to the group as 'us' including herself, and we loved her all the more for it. She could easily have distanced herself from the lower ranks. Instead, she treated us all as though we were her equal. She kept an emotional distance though, her thoughts very much her own most of the time.

She boarded the train first, a large bag over her shoulder. The pilots followed, and the navigators after them. I gave Sophia a smile before stepping off the platform and into a warm carriage.

It was nothing fancy, just a troop transport, dim and smelling faintly of human odours; sweat and urine. I wrinkled my nose but went to sit beside Inna. Already past thirty, the woman was one of the oldest of our group and already a navigator. She never had an unkind word to say about anyone and most of us looked up to her like a mother or a big sister. Her brown hair had already turned grey at her temples, but that only served to make her look more kindly.

"Well, isn't this exciting?" she asked, putting her bag down at her feet. "And warm. Thread anyone?" She reached into her bag and pulled out several spools and needles.

I gave her a questioning look. "Thread? For what?"

She laughed, "For your uniform of course. You'll want to take it up, no?"

"Yes." We'd all been stumbling around in them for days. "Maybe we could use the extra fabric to bind around our feet, to make our boots fit?" I took a spool and needle and got scissors from my old suitcase.

I peeled my coat off first, glancing up to see the carriage doors slide shut. I hoped for a last glimpse at Moscow before the train started rolling from the station, but all I could see was darkness, broken only occasionally by the flash of a torch. I may never see my home or family again. The thought saddened me, although I wouldn't have hopped off the train even if Raskova told us we could. My place was here, with these women, to prove to myself and everyone, that I was willing to die to defend my motherland.

I felt Inna pat my arm and I looked over to her in time to see a wistful expression on her face as well. Glancing around, the other navigators had similar expressions on theirs, a mixture of trepidation and determination. Almost as one, we bent our heads to our work. As I started to trim my coat sleeves, I started singing softly, "Vniz po matushkye po Volgye, po Volgye, po shirokomu razdolyu, razdolyu. Down the Volga, Mother Volga, over the wide sheet of water…"

A few moments later Inna started singing as well, then Valentina Yazova, one of the mechanics who was sharing our carriage. A few others joined her and before long, we were all singing and sewing as the train chugged through our poor, war-torn country.

"The train has stopped again." From my doze, I heard Valentina's voice. I yawned and sat up.

"It might be easier if you told us when it was moving." Sophia had joined us in our warmer carriage and had been snoring moments earlier.

I laughed at her reply, but she was right. Our train had had to be stopped repeatedly to let other trains pass. Supplies for the front; fresh troops; weapons and ammunition trains; they had all rolled past us.

I peeked through a grubby window, but only saw a blur moving past. It thundered along, shaking us all in its wake. Several minutes passed and another went by. Then it was silent.

I rubbed my back and pulled my coat up over my shoulders. I was using it as a blanket, although I now regretted having trimmed its length. It would have covered my feet before, instead of falling to just above my ankles. We'd been on the train for five days now and were all anxious and dirty, and often cold. The human odours I'd smelt as I'd first boarded the train were nothing compared to the smell now. I'd have dearly loved a hot bath and to wash the tangles from my hair. At least everyone looked equally unkempt.

Almost everyone, anyway. Lillya Litviak had tailored her uniform to perfectly fit her tiny body. Her shirt was cinched tightly at her waist with a belt and her hair still looked immaculate. She looked more like a movie star than a pilot. I'd have marvelled even more if she'd managed to tailor her boots; but she still walked with more dignity than I ever would.

I sat up and rubbed my eyes, then took another look through the window. We had stopped in a very small station; I had no idea where. The flat land stretching out told me nothing. A tiny building, little more than a shack, had no writing on it that I could see. I doubted we'd reached our destination, but how much longer we had, I couldn't guess.   Across the track was a wooden wagon, full to the top with cabbages. Not exactly my favourite food, but they looked inviting after five days of existing on bread and herring. My stomach rebelled at the idea of eating either of them again. But cabbage…

I pushed my coat aside and slowly rose to my feet, my hand running silently up the wall.

"Nadia, what are you doing?" Inna asked, looking up at me, a slight frown marring her features.

I put a finger to my lips. If I got caught doing this, I might get shot, or worse, kicked off the train.

I hurried over to the door and slid it open, wincing at the heavy scraping noise it made. I glanced quickly at the carriage the pilots were travelling in, but no one came to see what was amiss.

"Nadia…" Inna warned slowly. "Don't…"

"Shhh," Valentina cut her off. "Come on, I'll help you." She must have seen the wagon as well, because she was right behind me, grinning broadly. Sophia was behind her and a few others as well.

My heart pounding, I slipped out between the gap in the door and onto the tracks. A glance left and right and I bolted across the tracks. There was no one around, not even to guard the wagon. I leaned over the side and reach inside. I grabbed a cabbage in either hand and ran back to the train.

Giggling, a handful of others followed, grabbing as many as they could. I threw mine to the girls waiting in the carriage and went back for more. On my second trip, I took bites out of one cabbage, as if I were a rabbit in a farmer's field. The vegetable had never tasted so good. I could have sat down and eaten the whole thing in moments.

Around me, the other women were crunching into theirs. We all sounded like bunnies, except for the occasional groan of happiness for the unlikely rare treat. You'd have thought they'd found a wagon of freshly baked pastries or ice cream.

With slightly guilty pleasure, I climbed back onto the train, only to come face to angry face with Militsa Kazarinova, Major Raskova's second in command.

I swallowed and almost choked on the bite I'd just taken.

"Put it back," she said. Her voice was low but colder than the tundra. She turned to the other girls and yelled, "Put it back, all of you! Now!"

The sudden rise in her voice made me start. I jumped so fast I almost fell backwards onto the track. I ran even faster to return the cabbage than I had to take it in the first place. We all did. Both Sophia and Valentina and the other girls with vegetables in their hands had faces that looked like thunder. I knew what they were thinking; we were hungry, even though the cabbages were clearly not intended for us.

I wanted to crawl under the carriage and hide until it left without me. It was over for me; I was going to be kicked off the train.

Swallowing tears of shame, I walked back to the doorway and looked up. At so many moments in life you think things can't get worse, but then they do; this was one of those. Standing beside Lieutenant Kazarinova was Major Raskova herself. Not only had I shamed myself, I'd shamed my idol as well. She wasn't looking at me though. She had a hand on Kazarinova's arm and was speaking to her, her voice too low for me to hear. Whatever she was saying, Lieutenant Kazarinova wasn't happy about it. From what I'd seen of the woman, she was rarely happy about anything, although she wouldn't be in her position if she wasn't an exceptional airwoman. She may not have been well liked, but we trusted Raskova's judgement implicitly. If she thought the woman belonged with us, then she did.

They stepped aside as I approached, both sets of eyes now firmly on me. I wilted in front of them and swallowed hard.

"Major Raskova, I'm so…"

"Please sit down, the train will be leaving soon." Her voice was deceptively soft, but I could see the disappointment on her face.

I lowered my eyes to the floor and went back to my seat. I swore to myself then and there that I'd never do anything to make her look at me like that again. I'd find a way to make her proud and not regret having chosen me.

Deep down though, my stomach was thanking me for my actions. Just that little bit of fresh vegetable buoyed me. Maybe I could survive on bread and herrings for a few days more, although I wouldn't stop dreaming of my mother's borscht with every monotonous mouthful.

CHAPTER 5

It was the middle of the night, raining and freezing cold when we finally pulled into a station and clambered sleepily from the train. A small sign dangling from a post told me that we had arrived at Engels Train Station. I had never been to Engels, or anywhere this far from Moscow, but I knew it was a town near the Volga River. Geography had been a favourite subject of mine at school.

Beyond the platform, fog hung so low I couldn't see more than a few steps in front of me. The rain fell softly, just enough to dampen anything or anyone in its path. From the look of the puddles on the road, it had been raining for hours, maybe days, but the weather hadn't been cold enough to turn the rain to snow. It was a small mercy for which I was very grateful.

No one had turned up at the station to greet us, which visibly irked Major Raskova. Who she had been expecting in the middle of the night, I wasn't sure. She left us standing on the platform and hurried off, returning a few minutes later with a yawning man.

"I'll call the base," he said, upon seeing about three hundred cold, tired and hungry women standing on his platform.

"Please," Raskova nodded, looking her usual serene self again. I had spoken to her only once since the 'cabbage incident', as Sophia kept jokingly referring to it. She had been going around to every girl in the nine days we were on the train, speaking to each at length about a variety of topics. When she came to me, I was scared she was going to chastise me, but she merely asked about my parents and my college studies.

"I lived with my mother," I had told her. "I was studying to be a teacher. I like children, but defending them seemed more important than teaching them right now."

"Will you go back and finish your studies after the war?" It seemed important to her. She'd sat on the edge of her seat and looked at me intently.

26

I hadn't thought about after, so it took me a few moments to respond. "Yes, I think I will."

Raskova nodded and smiled. "Good, it's important for all of us women to be involved in rebuilding after the war. We must not forget life does not end with victory. Everyone must go and be busy and contribute or all of this fighting is for nothing." She had such great foresight and passion. I wanted to ask what she'd do after the war, but I didn't dare. I think I could have asked her about anything but her private life.

"Yes, Major Raskova," I replied instead. "I want to do my part."

She smiled at me again and patted my arm. "Of course you do, and you will." She'd left then and moved to speak to someone else, always showing the same level of interest in everyone.

I wasn't fooled though. I knew she hadn't forgotten what I'd done. I suspected she knew, and she also knew I wouldn't let her down again. Her faith in me only heightened my opinion of her. She commanded respect, but she also gave it in return. That, to me, was the mark of a true leader. If she commanded one of our regiments, I wanted to be in hers, but the competition would be stiff.

By the time several trucks arrived to collect us, I was shivering. I wanted to dive into the back of one and huddle up under cover. However, the pilots were allowed on first, as before, and the rest of us had to wait in the cold until they got settled. By the time I climbed up into the truck, I could barely feel my toes. I settled down beside the closest woman and put my suitcase down beside me.

"Are you trying to sit on me?"

I glanced over to my left and wanted to move and sit elsewhere. It was too late. Lena Turova glared at me, squashed as she was between me and another pilot. "Sorry," I muttered, moving a hand spanner away from her. I was shoved back though, by the rest of the girls piling into the small truck. Inna Markova squeezed in on my other side and almost ended up on her lap. I had nowhere to go though and could only turn to her, virtually nose to nose, and give her a wry look, which she returned, with a smile. I could hardly breathe during the whole ride, but at least I was warm.

"You think they'd organize more trucks," someone said loudly. I don't know who voiced that out loud. I wouldn't have dared.

After a few minutes, feeling returned to my toes, although my ribs were pressed uncomfortably and my arms could barely move. Through the press I could see Sophia, who had the advantage of being able to see over all of our heads. She'd made herself as small as she could, which wasn't easy, considering her size.

Every bump in the road made the truck bounce, which hurt my rear. By the sound of the groans every time we went over one, everyone else was feeling it as well. After a particularly nasty one, I glanced over at Lena. Rather than complain, as I might have expected, she was gritting her teeth. It was hard not to have some respect for her, until she made a rude face at me and looked away.

"Don't worry about her, she'll come around," Inna whispered into my ear. She always saw the best in people, even people like Lena.

"And if she doesn't?" I asked, well aware Lena could probably hear us. The way her jaw was set, angrily, she was listening.

"Then it won't be your problem. Worry about the fascists."

I couldn't help myself, I snorted softly. Of course, they were the enemy here, not Lena, not any one of us. I just hoped the pilot remembered that as well.

Engels Air Force Base looked old and tired. It was surrounded by sandbags, piles of them, out of which stuck anti-aircraft guns. Red Army soldiers manned the perimeter; several of who stepped forward as the trucks stopped and we climbed off.

"Papers." The order was brisk, but had probably been delivered to hundreds, maybe thousands, of airmen over recent months and years.

I reached into my bag for mine and handed them to the soldier standing beside the gate. He looked them over, nodded and handed them back before holding his hand out to the woman behind me.

Assuming that was a dismissal, I walked though the gates.

Marina Raskova was herding us toward the old Red Army Gymnasium, but like everyone else, I looked around while I walked. The sun had risen enough to see rows of Po-2 biplanes lined up and ready to be used to train us. The sight of them was reassuring, as were the familiar smells of aircraft, balancing out the unease of being surrounded by armed men in what must be a prime target for the enemy.

"Hey, you survived!" Sophia's voice boomed over the low chatter of the other girls. She carried her bag over to walk beside me, droplets of the slow, cold rain dripping from her nose.

"I saw you stuck beside Turova."

"She doesn't like me." I rolled my stiff shoulders and neck. Surely the fact I was here at all should be an indication I was considered competent and useful.

Sophia made a rude noise. "Lena Turova doesn't like anyone, including herself."

"Now, now girls," Inna scolded. "She's not so bad."

"Not so bad?" Sophia asked, her blue eyes wide. "How can you—"

"Attention please, ladies." Marina Raskova's soft voice shushed us all. We turned to her as she gestured toward the gymnasium. "We'll be staying in here while in training at Engels. It's been converted into a dormitory expressly for our use. It won't be glamorous." She smiled at her own words. "But it will suit our needs. Go inside and get some sleep. You'll be up at dawn. Now the hard work begins."

She was as good as her word, of course. We were woken at dawn and expected to be dressed in our full, and better fitting, uniforms within five minutes.

Dressing was easy enough, but it took time for me to strap my feet so they didn't swim in my boots. I glanced around the room I shared with Sophia, Valentina and a pilot, Antonina Palova. We had one of the warmer rooms, so a couple of other girls had crept in and slept on the floor. I wasn't much more comfortable on my tiny, lumpy bed than they would have been on the hard tiles, but they were welcome to share the warmth.

Sophia was dressed already, her large feet snugly pressed into her boots. Valentina and Antonina were winding fabric around their feet as fast as they could manage.

"I need a bath," Antonina commented, wrinkling her nose in the vicinity of her own armpit.

"We all do," I agreed. Nine days in close quarters on the train with no way to wash hadn't made any of us pleasant. Hopefully there was a bath on the base, or somewhere close. I tucked my bindings into themselves and shoved on my boots. I was sure it had been longer than five minutes, but I'd taken less time than some of the others. I waited for them all to be ready before we all turned out, standing in lines outside the gym, hands clasped in front of us.

A few men walked past us and snickered. "Women, playing at being air force," one of them muttered. "Can't even turn out properly."

I glanced around and realized with despair — they were right. Our lines were messy and some of the girls hadn't finished dressing. The girl behind me was still tucking her shirt into her pants. No wonder they were laughing. I felt myself going red in the face. It had taken long enough to be allowed to fight, without making ourselves a laughing stock on the first day.

There was a shuffle as girls adjusted their clothing and moved to make neat, straight lines. By the time Major Raskova appeared in front of us, we were a little more presentable. I couldn't tell by the look on her face whether she'd seen us before, or heard the men speaking. I had a feeling if she'd done the latter, she'd have been unruffled, but more determined to make us succeed than she already was.

"We'll turn out faster tomorrow," she declared. "We have a lot of work to do, but first, we must make airwomen out of you. You'll all be getting your hair cut, boy length."

I gasped, my hand reflexively going to my long, brown hair. It had taken years to grow and I was immensely proud of it. Well, perhaps not now, dirty as it was. Still, it could be washed, brushed and put back into its plait.

I did wonder, perhaps insolently, if 'all' included Major Raskova. She had hers tied up in neat plaits and pinned up under beret, but it'd be a shame to cut it, as it would any of our hair.

All around me, the other women were muttering, outraged at the very idea. Antonina was looking stony faced, her hands crossed over her chest. Only Sophia looked unperturbed.

"And the first to have her hair cut will be…" Raskova's voice silenced the group, her eyes scanning the crowd. I had a sinking feeling until her eyes settled on me.

"Nadia Valinsky." Oh, she had not forgotten the cabbage incident.

For a moment, I was resigned to accept my punishment, knowing all of the girls would be staring at me and laughing at me, before their turns came. Then I realised something. This was meant as something more, a test perhaps. I could prove to Major Raskova I could take what was dished to me, and do it with dignity.

Raising my chin, I looked at her, right in her eyes. "Yes ma'am," I replied, my voice even and firm. I stepped out of the line and followed her to the barbers, near the gymnasium. The rest of the women followed, solemnly, but Sophia and Valentina fell in beside me.

"We took the cabbages too," Sophia pointed out. "It's only fair we go next, after you."

"Yes," Valentina agreed cheerfully. "Besides, it's only hair, it'll grow back."

"Tell that to Antonina," Sophia replied.

I glanced back over my shoulder. The pretty pilot with long blonde hair had tears trickling down her face and she wasn't the only one. Lillya Litviak looked very unimpressed, although a cut would save her a lot of rubles in peroxide. Lena Turova was scowling at the back of Marina Raskova's head and Inna Markova was weeping softly.

"Right, " I muttered. "It's only hair."

CHAPTER 6

"We're approaching the target!" I called through the plane's intercom. I hardly needed to tell her. We'd done this over the practice grounds near the base so many times before, we both knew where we were, but as navigator it was my job to communicate this kind of information to her. Even in practice, there was no place for complacency. At the front, that could get us killed. As it was, we were getting years worth of training in half a year, so we wouldn't cut any extra corners.

My training days were fourteen or fifteen hours long. Those of us chosen as navigators rose an hour before everyone else. We'd dress and have a class of Morse code then join everyone else for exercise and drills before breakfast. Then we'd have ten more classes in navigating, and combat flying and after that we'd do aerial drills. These, of course we enjoyed the most.

The engine of our Polikarpov Po-2 biplanes, the aircraft in which we trained, made a pleasant popping sound, which reminded me of my mother's sewing machine. The wind was always bitterly cold, rushing past my face. The open cockpit offered no protection from the bitterness of winter. Even with a helmet, goggles, a warm coat and thick gloves, I was still cold. I could feel my cheeks turning red and dry, but I was never going to complain out loud. We'd volunteered to be here; we could leave any time we chose to, but no one wanted to leave involuntarily, in spite of our haircuts.

I had had a habit of twirling my hair around my finger when I was agitated. Now my hair was so short, I kept on reaching for it and then scratching my ear, as if that was my intention all along. It was becoming something of a nervous tic. I was often anxious, but usually too exhausted to be nervous. When we were flying, I toyed with the excess leather on the side of my flight goggles. I had to force myself to lower my hand, to steady the map and compass on my lap.

I looked at the back of Antonina's head, wisps of the blonde's hair sticking out from under her helmet. She'd flatly refused to let anyone cut her hair and somehow, she'd been allowed to keep it long.

Perhaps this was simply because Marina Raskova hadn't cut her hair, so she hadn't the heart to insist we all do it. In any case, the breach in regulations hadn't seemed to matter; we'd been allowed to let our hair grow out in the months since we'd arrived at Engels. Of course we had to keep it tied back or tucked under a hairnet, but we preferred that to looking like the boys.

I suspected the reason they'd made us have it cut was to remind us of our equality. No one was the prettiest or the blondest or the darkest. We were all comrades, all trainees. It had been a timely, if traumatic, reminder for some of us.

"Understood," she replied cheerfully. The plane banked gently as we soared low over the target. We'd all had a problem hitting them. The Po-2 having not been made for this, had no bombsights, so we'd all started off having to guess when to drop them.

Some of the group had been so far off the mark it was lucky the ground below us was uninhibited, or someone might have lost a life or a home.

Today though, we were trying something different. After so many misses, Antonina had commented, "We're all different heights, so if we're looking for the same part of the wing to pass over the target before we drop, then of course they'll be different. We're all seeing the wings from different angles."

"What do you suggest then?" Evdokiia Bershankskaia had asked. The woman was one of the most experienced and older pilots among us and we all respected her.

I watched Antonina thinking frantically. "If there's a point on the wing where, after it passed over the target, we'd know to drop," she'd said slowly. "But that point will be different for us all, so we can't use a fixed point like a strut. We all need our own reference point on the wing—"

I could see her coming to some sort of conclusion and felt myself grinning. I had some idea of what she was about to suggest, but the blank faces around me suggested the others hadn't got it yet.

"What if we put a mark on the wing for each girl, in just the right place?" Antonina said triumphantly. "Maybe with chalk to start with?"

Now Evdokiia was smiling as well. "Let's try it."

Much to Antonina's pleasure, it worked perfectly. Some of the girls grumbled, at first. They wished they'd thought of it, or believed our superiors should have, but they adopted the idea and landed their targets with greatly increased precision.

Other girls even stopped complaining it was unfair that Antonina got to keep her hair.

Of course the chalk markers were only helpful to the pilot. The navigators could only sit in the back and watch once we'd reached the target, but it was still thrilling to be airborne.

"Bombs away!" Antonina called cheerfully. I saw her pull the release and watched the bombs fall away and hit, sending up a cloud of smoke and a spray of mud.

In the sky, working together, we could almost forget the war; until the wheels hit the runway of the air force base and the armourers would run to reload the bombs. The mechanics would refuel the plane and off we'd go again. In the evenings, the mechanics would tug the plane over to a handstand and tie it down for the night.

*****

On the walks back across the field, past dozens of planes and men and women training to fight, I'd remember why I was there. And yet, in spite of all our work, we were still a novelty; still the pretty canaries many men thought to be frivolous and useless.

"Are you really going to fight?" some of the men would call as I walked past. "Hey, I'm going to the front tomorrow, you could give me one last night of fun before I die."

"If you're going to the front," I'd call back, "you should get some sleep, then maybe you won't die. Then you can go back to your wives."

The men, most of them no more than boys, would laugh and whistle at me. All except for one. He had the deepest, darkest brown eyes I had ever seen. He wasn't as handsome as some of the other men, but I could have drowned in those eyes. Every now and again, he'd glance at me and then look away. His apparent disregard disappointed me, even though it was easier to watch him when his eyes were turned away.

"Who is he?" I asked Sophia one day. She seemed to know the names of every man and woman on the base, where they'd come from and where they were going, and if they were heading to the front soon.

"Nikolai Levkin," she replied, once she'd looked to see which 'he' I was referring to. "He's training to fly the Sturmovik. They're waiting for more to arrive before they go to the front."

I was impressed. I'd seen a few of the Ilyshin-IL2, Sturmovik, or Stormtrooper, around the base. 'Flying tanks', they were called. Heavily armoured and with the best weaponry, and room for a rear gunner, they were rumoured to be both very effective and difficult to fly.

I'd be more likely grow wings than be allowed to fly one myself, at least for now.

"I don't think he likes me," I said. "He ignores me whenever the others are talking to me, or he looks away." I was staring at him, but I didn't care.

"Hey Kolya." One of his friends referred to him in the diminutive form of his name before nudging him in the ribs with their elbow, his finger pointing in my direction.

Nikolai's gaze rose until he was looking right at me. Then he blushed and looked away.

"See?" I sighed. I heard Sophia chuckle and glared at her.

"I think he likes you too much. Go and talk to him." She raised her hand to give me a shove, but I ducked away.

"No, I couldn't." Especially with his friends watching and laughing.

I kept walking, back toward the old gymnasium. Just before I was out of sight, I glanced back over my shoulder.

Nikolai was staring at me. As before, he glanced away as soon as he realised I was looking.

I heard a roar of laughter from his friends, and something about 'women pretending to be pilots'; I knew it hadn't been Nikolai speaking.

I had never heard his voice, but I was sure he wouldn't make fun of us. If anything, he seemed too serious for that.

The train from Saratov to Engles rattled on the tracks. The land visible out the window was flat, bathed in a red-gold glow; the last of the rays of the sun. The smoke in the air made for striking sunsets; a stark reminder life went on in spite of the war. A giggle made me turn my head and look down the dusty carriage. Every ten days, my whole regiment would take the train to the town across the Volga to use the bathhouse there. For us, it was akin to a holiday; it was a chance to be girls again.

The men would go as well, but we'd hang sheets between us, so they couldn't see us. We could hear them joking, and we'd laugh at the silly things they said.

It made me uncomfortable at first, having them so close, but the chance to be clean made me quickly forget.

With clean hair and skin, we'd sing all the way back to Engels and many of the girls would flirt with the boys. Most of the men were at least half in love with Lillya Litviak, who didn't seem to be interested in any of them.

"I'd marry my aircraft before I'd marry any of them," I heard her declare from several seats ahead.

I smiled, but I almost believed her. Her love of acrobatics was famous, actually infamous now, since technically she wasn't supposed to do it in our training aircraft and not so low to the ground.

That didn't stop her though. She'd always looked contrite afterward, but I don't think anyone believed she really was, and she never stopped anyway. She always got away with the most outrageous manoeuvres, I think because she was so skilled they knew she'd be needed. She was also smart enough to behave in front of anyone of high enough authority to ground her for the rest of the war, and good enough that none of the trainee navigators complained about flying with her. Some did come back with white faces occasionally, but never said a word against Lillya.

At any rate, I don't think she thought men were anywhere near as fun as barrel rolls, so they had to settle for the occasional kind word or smile from her.

Some of the men had made good friends with some of the girls, although we had little time for more, and after our studies, even less energy.

No one showed any real interest in me, apart from joking around. That was fine. I only had eyes for one man, who apparently hardly noticed or cared I existed. I sighed softly and looked over to where Sophia sat, deep in conversation with another armourer. He seemed sweet and only had eyes for her, but she was all business with all of the men. I don't think she even noticed the looks he gave her. I would have to ask her about that later. In the meantime, they made a charming couple.

"Do you mind if I sit here for a moment?" A male voice interrupted my thoughts.

I turned my head and there he was, those big brown eyes looking at me, sitting beside me.

"Please?" Nikolai asked, looking like a dog when it's hoping for a special treat.

"Yes, I mean no. I mean, I don't mind." Of course I would trip over my own tongue, I'd been wanting to speak to him for weeks.

He smiled and for a moment I thought he'd laugh at me, like his friends did. He didn't. His smile was warm and relieved. How could he not know I'd have told him yes? Of course, he couldn't read my mind, but hadn't I been staring enough?

"Good, I've been wanting to talk to you," he admitted. "I come from a very small village, so I'm not used to talking to people I don't know. And you being from Moscow, you must be used to boys who are much more sophisticated than I am."

My heart skipped a beat. "How did you know I was from Moscow?" I asked. My accent perhaps?

"I…" Nikolai blushed. "I asked around."

If he'd said he'd broken into Raskova's office and looked me up in her files, I wouldn't have been more surprised. Hopefully he hadn't done that as well though.

"Oh, you did? I…did the same thing." And I blushed, his face reddened once again. Together we had enough colour in our faces to match a good bowl of borscht.

He cleared his throat, his expression suddenly regretful. "Our aircraft arrived. You probably saw them?"

I had. We all had. Not a single one amongst us girls hadn't sighed at the idea of flying a Sturmovik. Our poor old Po-2s looked like ageing grandparents beside them.

I nodded and let him continue.

"I'm leaving for the front in the morning."

My heart sank a little as I jumped to the conclusion he might want one night of fun with me before he left.

I opened my mouth to retort that I had no intention of letting any man use me just because they might die tomorrow.

"I was wondering if I could write to you." He looked at me earnestly and I felt terrible for jumping so quickly to such a conclusion.

I slammed my mouth shut before something silly came out.

"Write to me?" I asked, after a few moments.

"Yes. I know it's taken too long to let you know I'm interested in you, but maybe if we write, then when the war is over—" He shrugged. "I don't expect any promises, but I think getting letters from you might help get me through to the end."

Strange as it may sound, it was the most romantic thing I'd heard in my life, up until then.

"So…can I?"

"Yes," I answered, finally. "I'd like that. Very much."

As the train drew into the station, he leaned over and kissed my cheek. It was very chaste, almost brotherly, but the memory of his lips on my skin would keep me going for a long time.

CHAPTER 7

Missing someone I barely knew was a strange sensation, but what I felt as I tried to sleep that night. Nikolai and I had talked the whole way back to Engels; sharing how scared we were, but how proud we were to be defending our motherland, talking about my brothers and his sisters. His parents had died when he was young, leaving him and his two older sisters to live with an aunt too old to manage three energetic children.

We parted reluctantly at the station to the teasing of his friends. As if they hadn't been flirting with my friends only minutes earlier.

"Kolya has a girlfriend!" they taunted childishly. "Kolya is in love! Did you kiss her? Do we have to stay out of our room tonight?" He took it all with good humour, mostly ignoring their jibes. He glanced at me, but he was too much of a gentleman to ask. I felt bad for having doubted that about him, but I don't think he blamed me for presuming it. The boys had been trying to get girls alone for weeks.

Luckily, none of the girls teased me, nor did they seem jealous or the least bit annoyed that the young man with such lovely eyes had paid attention to me. Sophia, Antonina, Valentina and Lillya were happy for me, although Lillya did give me a funny look.

"I don't know why you'd want to bother with any of them, when you're so young, but if you're happy, then I'm happy," she'd declared.

That was the difference between us girls and those boys. It made me glad I was in a women's regiment and not a mixed one, as some women in the front already were. I wouldn't have wanted to put up with the crass comments and derisive looks on a regular basis.

I went to bed that night with a smile on my face, but it didn't last long. An hour after midnight, I was awoken by a loud alarm, blasting through the whole dormitory like an air raid warning. The sound was piercing and immediately brought everyone to complete wakefulness. With only a moment of hesitation, because I'd really rather have been in bed sleeping, I got up, stripped off my nightgown and dressed in my full uniform, including my ridiculously oversized boots.

I combed my hair with my fingers and pulled on my hat. To my surprise, Sophia was already at the door waiting for me.

Antonina, who didn't do very well at waking up suddenly and having to dress, was doing her best to hurry.

"Maybe if your hair was short, it'd take less time," Sophia teased her, miming scissors cutting with her fingers. She grinned and wiggled her eyebrows playfully at me. I grinned back and mimed holding out Antonina's pretty hair for cutting.

"Be quiet," Antonina snapped, plaiting her hair quickly and tying it up. "I'm not letting them cut it!"

I couldn't help but laugh, which earned me a glare from the pilot. I stuck my tongue out at her and hurried toward the door. I wasn't going to keep Major Raskova waiting. I didn't dare.

No one did. We formed up in neat lines, side by side directly behind each woman in front of us, our hands clasped neatly, eyes forward. Mine followed Raskova, just a little bit, wondering, as she inspected us, when she'd started to look so tired. She had little lines around her eyes and mouth and a grey hair or two at her temples. She was only 30 years old.

She stopped first at Lillya Litviak, an eyebrow raised at the younger pilot. "What is on your collar?" she asked, looking more amused than annoyed.

"I was up all night taking the collar off my coat and sewing on this furred one. The fur came from the top of my boots," Lillya replied unrepentantly.

"Well then," Raskova replied, "you won't mind being up all night sewing the regulation collar back on then."

Lillya simply smiled, like a child who knew they wouldn't get away with something naughty, but had tried it anyway, just in case. Secretly, I thought her collar was a great improvement and would have liked to do the same myself, but uniforms were uniforms.

A slight roll of her eyes for Lillya's temerity and Raskova moved on, nodding at each woman as she passed them, including me. I let out a soft sigh of relief, which was silly, because I knew how to dress myself properly.

My relief faded as our commander stopped in front of Sophia. She regarded her for a long moment, her expression unreadable until she frowned, her blue eyes looking annoyed.

"Open your coat please," she requested, softly and politely, but curt enough to indicate she expected to be obeyed without question.

I turned my face and stared at her and at Sophia. I also frowned, confused as to why Raskova was asking this. It was certainly an unusual order.

Evidently, it was not so unexpected for my dearest friend. Sophia sighed and quickly unbuttoned her coat, just a few buttons, just enough for us all to see.

I gaped in disbelief. So that was why she'd been dressed so quickly. Instead of her uniform, she wore her nightdress under her long coat. She'd simply stuffed her feet into her boots and turned out with the rest of us. And me, so busy with my own uniform, hadn't noticed a thing.

"Anyone else?" Major Raskova looked furious, but she never, ever raised her voice and tonight was no exception. I had no doubt she'd go to every single one of us and check us all if no one else stepped forward. To my surprise and Raskova's all too evident disappointment, nine more women raised their hands and opened their coats to reveal their nightgowns.

It might seem like such a minor infraction, but it showed a terrible lack of discipline and made our attempts to prove ourselves as serious airwomen much less convincing. We had to do everything as well as, if not better than, the men. We had to fly well; land well; learn quickly; work hard; and be disciplined and professional. That meant following orders implicitly and following them well, not giving the men reason to doubt our desire or our abilities.

Besides, who would want to have to fly in the middle of the night while at the front, have to make an emergency landing and end up in a war zone in their nightgown? Getting up quickly and dressing fully was a very useful skill to have.

"All of you ladies who decided to take a short cut," Raskova said, addressing them all, "can go for a walk around the airfield." She gestured out behind her, into the freezing, blustery night.

"But Major Raskova, it's…" One of the other navigators, Mariya Serova, started to argue, but she was cut off by a look from Raskova and the rest of us. It was freezing, but she'd brought this on herself. Neither she, nor Sophia, nor any of the rest of them, would get any sympathy. In fact, as we stood in the cold and watched them walking, the wind blowing their nightgowns around the bare parts of their legs, they'd brought it on us as well. That they looked contrite when they returned, their hands and faces red with cold, did little to improve the mood of the rest of us.

We all trudged back into the dormitory. I didn't say a word to Sophia. She couldn't look at me either. I stripped off my uniform, put my nightgown back on and slipped back into a bed, which had gone cold.

Before I fell back into an exhausted sleep, I heard Antonina's angry voice.

"Next time, get dressed."

We didn't talk about it the next day, or indeed again until we were out at the front and needed something silly to laugh at. The next time we all had to turn out in uniform for other than our morning drills, we were all immaculate. Of course, this was a momentous day. November 7th, 1941, the anniversary of the Revolution and a day of rest.

I was nervous, because today was more than simply an important anniversary. I had to fight to keep from fidgeting as Major Raskova and several important dignitaries, medals pinned to their chests, stood before us. Raskova was wearing her star, the Hero of the Soviet Union medal, which I hoped to be worthy of myself one day.

The day was sunny, but cold. The parade ground looked as though it had been trodden by thousands and thousands of feet. I wondered how many of those had been female, and reasoned it wouldn't have been many. Doubtless, we were the first regiment consisting entirely of women to have stood here like this. The 122nd Aviation Group was our official title. Not very grand, but it filled me with unreserved pride. War might not usually be women's business, but it was ours.

I took a breath and spoke as one with the rest of my regiment as we gave the military oath. I swore to be honest; brave; diligent; skillful and honourable and, if need be, give my life for my motherland. I spoke the words as loud and clearly as I could, trying not to trip over my tongue, although I did when I promised to give my life if I had to. I don't think there was a woman there who didn't mean it, but who also didn't want to think about the possibility.

When the oath was done and we were sworn to serve, we stood very still as Major Raskova addressed us. Her face was solemn, more so than usual. Any sign she might have had of her tiredness from the constant training didn't show in her demeanour and I couldn't hear it in her voice; but I knew she must have been exhausted.

She was always present when the aircraft returned from night bombing practice. She was there when the day bombers practiced and she was there when the most experienced pilots shot down balloons released for them to train in air-to -air combat. When she slept was a mystery to us all. Perhaps she didn't sleep. None of us did all that much anyway.

According to Sophia, we would sleep when the war is over and we'd won.

In the meantime, I concentrated on what Major Raskova was saying. She was reading from notes, but I could see in her blue eyes she meant every word and she meant for us to listen and absorb them.

"Study persistently," she told us. "With perseverance, the examination will be held on the field of battle."

These were the last words I heard of her speech that day. They echoed through my mind, so years later I could still hear her cultured voice saying them. It was the very first moment I truly appreciated the reality of my situation and what I had not only volunteered for, but insisted upon.

I was training at an actual air force base, to fly— at least navigate— aircraft that would fight a real enemy who would fight with bombs, guns and grenades. I could die, or worse, be shot down and captured. I shuddered to think what would happen to a woman who was shot down in enemy territory. I swore to myself then and there to do everything I could to prevent that from happening.

Clapping broke me from my thoughts; Major Raskova had finished speaking. Belatedly, I joined in the applause and stood to attention as she walked away to speak to the other dignitaries.

For a few moments, I'd have loved to have been home, on my tiny bed, in my tiny room, with its peeling paint and with my mother nearby. I hadn't heard from her since I'd left Moscow, so I didn't know whether or not she was alive. The realisation that my world had changed so fully shook me. My motherland would be a different place for the next generation and the one after that. Not a fascist one, of that I was determined. I would study, I would persevere and I would pass Major Raskova's test.

CHAPTER 8

The months flew by, literally, some of the time. A lot of it became a blur of classes, drilling and routines. I'd find myself dreaming of odd things, like messages in Morse code. I'd gone over and over each letter, each word, so many times I could translate in my sleep. Of course, as is often the case with dreams, the messages made no sense. I'd dream of a recipe for cabbage soup that smelled like aircraft fuel and burned the tongue like fire. I dreamed that when we dropped bombs, they were pots of soup instead and the enemy would scream as their skin blistered. I'd dream of getting messages from home which told me my pet cat had died. That was strange; I hadn't had a cat since I was seven.

And I dreamed of Nikolai. Those were dreams I never remembered later, but I could feel the sensation of his kiss on my cheek and I'd blush.

Some nights, I'd go to bed with a headache, as though my brain couldn't handle all the new information without having to expand to fit it in. Some days I'd wake with a headache, as if anticipating a long, difficult day. Occasionally I'd find myself muddling up information I'd learnt in one class, with what I'd learnt in another. I was far from the only one to do that, but so far no major disasters had arisen from our mistakes. After all, plotting a course on a map had yet to endanger anyone.

In the long run, however, it would matter. My mistakes haunted me and made me determined not to make more.

"We're taking three years worth of training in six months," Antonina pointed out wearily.

Several of us were sitting at a long table in the mess hall, trying to fit in a hasty lunch between classes. The table looked tired from many years of use by many exhausted aviators.

"They can't afford to wait too long for us to be ready," I pointed out.

"In three years, the war might be over," Sophia replied, muffled.

I looked over to her, too tired to be horrified. "I hope it'll be less than that. It might even be over before we reach the front." I wasn't sure if I'd be more disappointed or relieved if that happened. No one wanted the war to continue, even if it meant all of our current labour was in vain.

"Then all of this would have been for nothing," Antonina groaned, flopping forward so her forehead pressed against the tabletop.

I opened my mouth to agree with her when Lillya Litviak spoke.

"Firstly, the war isn't going to end any time soon," she said. "They keep pushing us back. Since the only way for it to end soon is with our defeat, and that isn't going to happen, then we may have years more fighting ahead of us. And secondly, by being here and working so hard, and being incredibly impressive, we've proven we're as good as, if not better than, the men. Therefore, every single second here has been worthwhile."

When it came to flying, I doubted the diminutive woman lacked confidence. She'd been a part of a women's aerobatics team before the war. I had seen her perform once and she'd left me breathless. I didn't think there was anything she couldn't do in an aircraft. She worked hard daily, hourly, to gain and keep the respect of those around her. She deserved every bit of it. Even though she was shorter than I was, and the same age, I looked up to her, in many ways.

"And we look prettier," I joked.

"Yes!" Antonina agreed loudly, her voice carrying across the whole mess hall. The men, who had mostly gotten used to us girls by now, just smirked and shook their heads. They were sitting too far away to have heard my comment, so I'm sure they just thought 'silly girls' and went on with their meals.

Everyone at our table laughed.

"Except for our boots," I said, grimacing. "They're so big that when I turn around, they stay in the same place. Then I take a step and realise my boots are on backward. Major Raskova saw me the other day and she laughed." I had wanted to run away and hide, I'd been so mortified. Our boots weren't even the same lengths as each other.

Another of the women giggled and nodded her head. "I was working on a plane the other day and my boots got in the way so much that I took them off and worked with bare legs. It was so cold. And then I saw her coming and I had to jump back into my boots so fast, before she saw my uniform violation." Her eyes were huge with the memory, part horrified, part amused. Being caught would have meant time locked away in the guardhouse, which none of us wanted, but those boots were our bane.

"That's nothing," another of the women spoke up, her expression rueful. "I had to make a parachute jump today and first one boot fell off my feet and then the other. Even the wrappings I had to keep them on fell off. I don't know what was worse: the uniform violation or the worry they'd hit someone when they hit the ground. Of course then I had to get new ones and they were just as bad."

We laughed, but I caught the eye of Evdokiia Bershankskaia, who had been listening to us from another table. She had quickly become one of the women whose opinion Raskova respected.

For a moment I thought we might be in trouble for speaking up. Certainly our boots were ridiculous, but complaining about them, or anything, only made us look bad. I wished I hadn't said anything in the first place. Trust me to put my foot, boot and all, into my mouth.

I considered apologizing until Evdokiia spoke.

"Adjust them," she told us, just speaking loudly enough to be heard over the chatter of others in the hall. "I'll speak to Major Raskova about it."

That was how things were amongst us. We looked after each other. That was why, when it was announced there would be three regiments, we didn't mind who we'd be working with; it only mattered what job we'd be doing. Hands down, everyone wanted to be in the air fighter regiment. They would be actively fighting German planes in the air. Only the best of the best would be going into it. Lena Turova was convinced she'd be one of them and had told everyone this, in no uncertain terms.

"I am one of the best," I'd heard her say to Inna at breakfast one day. I was surprised she didn't claim to be the best, although I suspected she found Lillya's skills intimidating, as well as those of Raisa Beliaeva. Both of them would leave us all in the dust, even Major Raskova.

"Of course you are, dear," Inna had replied, without even a hint of mirth. "I'm sure you'll be right where you want to be." Why did the woman persist in stroking Lena's ego? She'd need to fly in an open cockpit just to accommodate it. There was nothing wrong with a healthy dose of self-confidence, but we were all supposed to be equals. The Germans certainly wouldn't be discriminating when they tried to shoot us down; Lena would be as big a target as the rest of us.

That was an unfair thought and I chastised myself for it. If you had skills, there was nothing wrong with being aware of it and using them. Hadn't our military oath told us so? And yet, being aware and bragging were so close to each other, it was sometimes difficult to tell them apart.

I nodded and smiled to Evdokiia and she smiled back. I wondered how she managed with all of us younger girls. At the start, when we'd arrived, she'd just been one of us. However, soon her age and experience, as well as her practical outlook on life, set her apart and above us. We'd look to her for guidance and advice and she'd always make time to give it.

Although some of us were in our early twenties, most of them were little more than a gaggle of teenaged girls. Silly ones too, at times. One of the pilots had been caught with perfume in the cockpit of the plane she'd been training in and many girls never came to the mess hall for meals without wearing lipstick. I didn't have any, so I couldn't wear it, but I think I would have if I'd been able.

Being able to fix our boots would do wonders for our morale. Maybe that was the point; keep us waiting until we needed a boost. If we could work in oversized boots then we could do anything.

"Major Raskova should have noticed before now," someone muttered behind me. I glanced around and saw Lena, but her mouth was closed and she turned away when she saw me. I couldn't prove who had spoken, but I was sure it was her.

Perhaps I did care a little bit who was in the same regiment as me.

*****

Some of the women received letters once or twice a week. Others got them less often, but it was always a cause for excitement when they arrived. For me, I hadn't had a single letter since I arrived at Engels. I had no word from my mother, nothing from any of my friends and no notifications of their deaths. I heard nothing of the brother whose life may or may not have already ended. Daily, worry gnawed at me a little more. I dreamed about their faces lying dead, their eyes staring like the dead dog I'd found in the street once, as a child. Would they smell putrid as well? The dream had turned my stomach over until I'd woken retching. I hadn't slept again that night.

I didn't need much; no long, sweeping letters detailing everything they'd seen, done and eaten since I'd left. No blow-by-blow descriptions of the war where they were. I needed none of that. Just a note saying they were alive and well would have sufficed and sustained me.

I kept my worries to myself. Everyone had his or her own problems without being burdened by mine. In a war, most people knew someone affected, who would be affected or who might be affected. More than one of the other girls had family in areas overrun by Germans and a few knew their loved ones were already dead. It made them angry and more determined to kill every fascist they could find.

Sophia, who seemed to get more letters than anyone, from all over our homeland, saw me wistfully looking at hers as we finished lunch.

"Still nothing?" she asked.

I looked at her in surprise; I thought I'd been so discreet. Then I suspected she'd noticed all along and had just waited until I was ready to talk about it. She might have been loud and brash, but she could be surprisingly sensitive.

"Not a thing. They might be dead…" Everyone I knew, everyone I'd grown up with, might be gone. My home might be a pile of rubble. The whole city might. None of that mattered. Buildings could be rebuilt. People…nothing could bring them back. I longed to hear my mother's voice urging me to marry and leave home, my father's asking for grandsons. I would have even liked to hear my brothers teasing my mercilessly for being a girl and wanting to wear my hair prettily and go to dances.

'Just because you both have two left feet,' I'd have retorted. 'And arms and legs too long for anything but tripping over them.'

They'd just laugh and call me a girly-girl, and put dead spiders in my bed.

Sophia put an arm around me and I leaned against her, silent tears falling freely, soaking the sleeve of her uniform.

"We're your family too," she said softly. "We're all sisters, soldiers; bound together for life. Even if we're not in the same regiment, we'll still be sisters, all of us. Even Lena." She wrinkled her nose. "We'll all write to each other and keep in touch. These last few months have welded us all together, haven't they?"

I nodded my agreement, but had no words in reply.

"They have," she declared. "We'll all be friends as long as we live."

Except we're going to the front and may die, I thought, so that might not be very long. I kept silent because the words were hanging in the air, daily. We lived and breathed them and worked to prevent them from happening. We were young and invincible and the German army should tremble in fear as our graduation day grew near, but they'd probably just laugh. Or they'd laugh at the idea of girls dropping bombs on them, expecting them to burst open and spray out flowers instead of death. They'd learn.

I sniffed and pulled a handkerchief out of my pocket. I gave a very unladylike blow of my nose into it and then wiped my eyes with the other side.

"I hope we're in the same regiment together," I said. "I like hearing all of the letters you get."

"I'll read the latest one then, shall I?" We should have been in class, but we took a few moments to listen to the exploits of a male friend of hers who had evacuated from Moscow and had just about travelled the length of our homeland on foot, to help other refugees find safe places to hide.

CHAPTER 9

Sophia and I had to run all the way, breathless with exertion, but inspired by the letter from her friend. Knowing there was still a world going on outside Engels, even a difficult world, made me more motivated to do well at my studies. Persist and persevere, Raskova's words echoed through my head over and over. The examination would come soon enough.

Before we even reached the classrooms, we saw the other airwomen, mechanics, armourers and support staff gathered around outside, shifting from foot to foot and mingling in the cold air. There was a buzz of excitement around the whole group, ripples of chatter passing back and forth through the waiting women.

I stopped beside Antonina just as Major Raskova appeared in the doorway, sheets of paper held in her hand. We didn't need to be told, or even looked at. As we'd practiced so many times before, we formed up into lines, everyone anticipating some announcement. That something important was taking place, there was no doubt in my mind. I had my suspicions, as did, I think, everyone else, but no one dared voice it out loud and I didn't even dare to think it.

I could feel my heart pounding. I was sure I could hear it as well; it was pumping so hard my chest hurt. Excitement radiated through the crowd, nervous laughter as someone accidentally stepped on someone else's foot. I bumped into the person beside me as I got into line and apologised, just as Antonina did the same to me. I smiled at her and she grinned back. She looked ready to dance out of her skin.

Major Raskova had that effect on us at times. She was so composed and poised I felt like a gangly schoolgirl in her presence. Days like this, when it was obvious something important was going to happen, it gave us all the jitters. I stood with my hands by my sides, tried to keep them still and focused, hoping the others would hurry up and do the same.

Raskova was visibly waiting for our silence and attention before she spoke. She cleared her throat, the silence was instant. "Very well then, ladies." She spoke only loud enough to be heard if we didn't make a sound. "We have been working hard to designate you all to regiments. We've taken into consideration your skills, abilities and personalities." She raised an eyebrow at Lillya Litviak, who looked totally unperturbed.

"I have in my hands the lists of who will be where." She paused for effect. The woman certainly knew how to have a group hanging onto her every word. "These assignments are not negotiable." She gave a stern look, her eyes sweeping across the crowd.

As if we'd have dared to argue.

"However," she continued slowly, her expression solemn, "I want you to remember you are volunteers. No one would think badly of you if you want to leave now." She paused to let us digest and respond.

We could go any time we wished, but if any girl did choose to go, now would be a good time to raise her hand and opt out.

No one made a sound, except a random cough from someone far to my left. It was no surprise to me not one woman even made a move.

By the expression on her face, I could tell Raskova was thinking the same thing. We'd all wanted this, even the long hours and hard work hadn't changed that. She gave a satisfied nod and gestured off to one side.

"If I call your name, you'll be in the 586th, the Fighter Aviation Regiment." She paused again as another ripple went through the group. Everyone woman wanted to hear her name, especially the pilots. I saw Lena standing a little taller, just in front of me. I hope she got what she wanted, I really did. Maybe then she'd be happy and stop deriding other people. But who else would be chosen? Surreptitiously, I scanned the group, or at least the ones I could see without moving my head too far.

"Your commanding officer will be Lieutenant Tamara Kazarinova." For some reason, the sides of Raskova's mouth tightened just slightly.

I didn't really know Kazarinova, but her sister had been the one who had caught us with the cabbages on the train. They were both career officers and very competent women, from what I'd heard. Tamara Kazarinova wouldn't have been chosen to lead if she wasn't able to do an exemplary job, I reasoned silently. In the end, we didn't have to like the person issuing the orders; we just had to follow them.

"Please move over there if I call your name." Raskova held up the first list and started reading. She began with Raisa Beliaeva, so I knew if she called my name I'd have to wait. I also knew Sophia wouldn't be in that regiment or her name would have been called first.

Eventually she reached the Ls.

"Lillya Litviak." No surprise there. The petite blonde all but skipped over to the new group, earning her an indulgent smile from Raskova. Lillya was beaming. I wanted to dance on the spot with happiness for her. Somehow, I managed to keep my feet still.

"Alexandra…" She went on for a minute or two, naming pilots, navigators, mechanics and support staff. When she was finished, there was a group of beaming women to one side, hugging and congratulating each other.

In front of me, Lena was glaring daggers at them all. I could only see the side of her face, but it was pink and her mouth was turned down in a scowl. Personally, I thought it strange she hadn't been chosen for the 586th, but doubtless our commanders had sound reasons for their choices.

"The next regiment will be designated the 588th Night Bomber Regiment. It will be very capably commanded by Senior Lieutenant Evdokiia Bershankskaia." I saw the two women look at each other. Raskova smirked and Evdokiia smiled ruefully.

I wondered why. Maybe she hadn't wanted to command, but I was happy for her. She'd do well in the role and the women in the regiment would follow her command and guidance almost as readily as we'd follow Major Raskova's.

Evdokiia stepped out of line to form the new group, her back straight, face looking bemused as Raskova started to read out a new list of names.

"Sophia Alanina, Inna Markova…"

I watched as, one by one, the women I knew, most of them my closest friends, moved over to stand proudly beside Evdokiia. As the list went on, I watched Valentina, Katya, Klavdia…person after person, name after name, walk away.

My heart slowed and felt heavier, as did my stomach. I wished I hadn't eaten so much lunch. My legs, which had wanted to dance moments earlier, now wanted to sag. I knew my expression was dour, because I could feel it and tried to adopt a mask of serenity, but I knew I failed miserably. If my heart wasn't serene, my face couldn't be.

"Antonina Yazova, Nadia Valinsky." When Raskova finally called my name, I thought I'd misheard. My heart skipped a beat and then went on pounding. The next thing I heard was Antonina laugh at the expression of surprise on my face. She gestured me over, grinning. I'd quickly lost the heavy feeling in my legs. Now, I wanted to scream or sing or dance, maybe all three. I hurried over, not wanting to delay the whole proceeding with my shock and delight.

I joined my regiment and turned in time to hear Lena's name called as well. Beside me, Sophia groaned, but I don't believe anyone was more upset than Lena herself.

Her face was red now, her mouth turned down in a scowl. She managed to square her back, march over to us and stand beside us, if a little way apart. I hoped she wouldn't give Evdokiia…Senior Lieutenant Bershankskaia, any trouble. I was already proud of our new regiment and didn't want myself or anyone else bringing shame onto us.

"The final regiment, you know who you are," Raskova concluded. "You are the 587th, the Day Bomber Regiment. Your commander will be…me."

We spontaneously broke into applause. The women who thought they'd been chosen last, might in fact have had the best of us all. They had the very great honour of being commanded by Major Raskova. Every one of them beamed with pride and I was happy for them. And for the sisters of my new regiment. And Lillya Litviak who would probably be doing cartwheels in an aircraft the moment she got to climb into one again.

"From now on, you'll be working in your regiments," Major Raskova continued. "You'll be assigned aircraft and a crew for each; one pilot, one navigator— where necessary and possible— as well as one mechanic and one armourer."

I knew that, even now, there weren't enough navigators, so some of us would be working twice as hard.

"588th, you will be drilling at night, so you're excused from drills right after class," Raskova added over the excited chatter.

I tried not to groan. I knew we'd be drilling all night. We'd need more practice than the other airwomen, because we'd need to use flares to light up targets and find landing areas, and we'd need to land in the dark. The planes would need to be refuelled and re-armed in the dark as well. Night raids might be a little bit safer than day ones, because it would be more difficult for the enemy to see us, but they were far from risk-free and certainly posed their own set of challenges.

"You're all dismissed. Now go and rearrange your sleeping quarters. Each regiment will reside together from now on."

I wanted to laugh at this, since Sophia, Antonina and I already shared a room. "Come on," Sophia said cheerfully, "we'll help you others to move."

*****

There was almost a festive feeling in the air that afternoon. The designation of regiments had made graduation seem that much closer. From being months away, we knew we were weeks, maybe days away from being sent to the front.

We sang and danced all the way back to the gymnasium, earning us a glare from one of the male trainers who was walking across the base. Some of the older men still didn't think we should be there, but as long as they didn't speak out against us, then we were polite and respectful to them.

Maybe the wave I gave him wasn't exactly respectful, or professional, but all the other women joined in. Nothing could dampen our good mood. We were still singing like a regiment of canaries when we reached the dormitory.

Our new commanding officers directed us on where to move to, with the night regiment housed to one side of the gymnasium and the day regiments on the other. We all helped to pack belongings and move everyone around.

There was a brief argument when two girls from one day regiment and two girls from another had been sharing a room. One woman started throwing clothing out the doorway and almost hit Valentina in the face with a boot. Sophia grabbed her arms and held her down on the floor while we tickled her mercilessly.

"After such a callous torture," Antonina declared, "I think she should stay in the room."

"Agreed!" I sang out loudly. "And anyone arguing will be subjected to tickling as well."

We stalked around the rooms, laughing and looking for potential victims. It came back on us though, when some of the girls from the 587th hunted us down and tickled us until we begged for mercy.

Finally everyone was settled, with Lena and Inna sharing a room with two other women from the 588th, while Valentina had moved in with Antonina, Sophia and I. Since ours was one of the warmer rooms, the members of the new 586th who had been sleeping on our floor were somewhat put out. However, orders were orders.

Silence reigned when the others went off to drills and we lay down to rest before night fell. I dozed a little and dreamed of Nikolai, piloting his Sturmovik into the clouds over a German camp. I awoke at sunset, wondering where he was and hoping he was all right. Even my worry over him and my family couldn't dampen my good mood and pride in my new regiment, so I pushed the thoughts away and dressed for the night's drills.

CHAPTER 10

I have to admit there was something exciting about drilling and working at night. I'd always been a bit of a night owl, so the regiment suited me well. The flying, especially the landing, could be tricky, but it felt as though we had the sky to ourselves on some nights, sharing it only with the stars. On others, when the moon was full, the Po-2s looked like bats against its luminosity.

Tonight was dark, with high cloud obscuring the moon and the stars. Only tiny lights showed us where the airfield was. Walking to it without bumping into anyone else or tripping over something became our first challenge.

"Hold hands," Antonina suggested.

"Good idea." With her voice, we wouldn't lose Sophia in the dark. She grabbed my gloved hand and I took a hold of Valentina's and we walked like that, a row of women, supporting each other as we went.

"Ouch!" Antonina's voice exclaimed. "I think someone left something lying around there."

"Oh no," Inna giggled. "That was my foot."

I couldn't stop myself from laughing; we were all laughing.

"I hope you don't do that at the front," Evdokiia Bershankskaia's voice came out of the darkness. "The fascists will hear you coming from so far away, they'll have their guns out before you know they're there."

"Sorry Senior Lieutenant Bershankskaia," we all said, accidentally in unison. "Senior Lieutenant Bershankskaia is it?" She sighed. "I suppose it is. All right, I have crew assignments for you."

So soon? I looked around, but could hardly see the rest of my regiment as it was. I smiled softly to myself.

If she heard it, our commanding officer gave no indication. "Antonina, Nadia, Sophia and Valentina, you four work well together, so I see no reason to change that."

I let out a squeal of delight before I could hold it back.

"Don't make me change my mind," Bershankskaia added, in a tolerant tone. She'd take a lot from us younger girls, but it wouldn't do to push her too far. We probably got away with too much as it was.

"Sorry," I muttered. "I mean, sorry ma'am."

I heard someone snicker.

"Sorry is fine," Bershankskaia sighed again.

"Lena and Inna, you're in a crew, together with…" She named everyone and had placed everyone with women with who they had already shown they could work well. Not once did she hesitate, which impressed me. She must have had everything worked out in her head. I knew I wouldn't remember everyone so effortlessly.

"And one last thing." Our commanding officer sounded less impressed with this than she did with the idea of leading us. "When we go to the front, we'll be flying Po-2s."

A groan of disbelief broke from between my lips, echoed by the girls around me.

"But they're so slow," someone, I think it was Anna Averin, complained.

"They have no weapons either and no parachutes." I thought that was Mariya Golova, a navigator.

"Nonetheless, these are what we'll be flying in," Bershankskaia replied patiently. "Now girls, to your planes please."

With just enough light to see the aircraft and the runway, we hurried over to the plane we'd been using. Sophia had jokingly named it Mat, 'mother', because she said it was old and slow, like hers. It was already fuelled and loaded with bombs so Antonina and I climbed aboard, me behind her in the double cockpit. The Po-2 was intended to be a training aircraft and had duel controls. Usually the trainer would have sat in the back and the trainee in the front. For our purposes though, we sat in what was technically reverse, although most of the navigators were also pilots.

I tugged my goggles down over my eyes and wriggled my nose to settle them. They weren't comfortable, but snow, rain and bugs in my eyes would be worse.

I felt the thrum of the engine as Antonina turned it on. Pop…pop pop pop. The Po-2's engine was a comforting sound, nothing like the roar of the Sturmoviks or even the PE-2s or Yak-1s. It wasn't that I thought we'd be flying Sturmoviks, but the Po-2 was like a donkey in a stable of thoroughbreds.

"Not very elegant, is it?" I asked, speaking to Antonina through the intercom.

"It's no flying tank," she called back. "But she can sideslip faster than…well, a balloon." She laughed.

I smiled, but the idea of being in the sky, at the front, and being basically defenceless, didn't exactly fill me with a sense of joy.

I felt the aircraft taxi toward the runway and decided to be glad we had one at all. Where I would have been without Raskova's regiments, I could only guess. Digging ditches somewhere else, or maybe dead? Not in a plane, of that I was certain.

My very favourite part of flying had always been the lift-off; that sensation of my stomach dropping, being left behind, while the rest of me rose. I knew some people loathed the feeling, but it gave me a thrill every time, even on a full stomach. This time was no different and I let out a spontaneous whoop of excitement.

I wasn't just Nadia, the student teacher from Moscow, anymore. I wasn't just my parent's daughter or my brother's sister. I was Nadia Valinsky, of the 588th regiment, one of Marina Raskova's girls.

The darkness spread out below us like a carpet of black velvet, occasionally dotted by lights below and stars above when there was a break in the clouds. Behind us, I knew my sisters were taking off, heading toward our practice target. Each plane would be three minutes behind the one before, so we'd have time to find the target, drop our bombs and circle back as the next plane approached.

I shone a torch on the map I had spread out across my lap, checking the route to tonight's target. I had a compass that I always checked twice, and a sextant with which I had become proficient. I'd have preferred an aircraft with its own navigation controls, but we'd make do. I hadn't gotten us lost yet. Of course that was more difficult when we had flown over the same ground a hundred times and knew every landmark; every haystack and small building; and the position of the stars. It was these I used now to guide us, factoring in the wind and angle from which we'd taken off.

"You're about ten degrees too far west," I said through the intercom.

"Thanks." Antonina adjusted our heading, banking the Po-2 gently eastward. "Can you find me a target please?"

"Yes," I replied. "Yes I can." I had to pull of my gloves, which meant several seconds of freezing cold hands. They were already shivering by the time I picked up a flare. I lit it and threw it out of the cockpit. Its tiny parachute caught in the breeze and opened out. The flare drifted downward slowly, illuminating the land below it, showing clearly where the target lay, below and a little in front of us.

"Bombs away!" Antonina called happily. She pressed the release and the doors on the bomb racks shifted slightly, but not enough to drop their load.

I held my breath and waited, but all I could feel was the thrum of the engine. This was a drill and we only carried ten kilogram bombs, but we should still feel a slight lift when they fell free. I'd felt it so many times I'd learned to wait for it without thinking. When it didn't come, I knew something wasn't right.

"Um…Nadia…"

I knew exactly what she wanted me to do, but I hesitated. I closed my eyes and took a deep breath. There would be no shame in not hitting our target if our equipment failed and I knew Antonina wouldn't blame me for balking. On the other hand, this could mean life or death on the battlefield. If I couldn't do this now, in a drill, then I wouldn't when it counted most. I swallowed hard and opened my eyes, scared but determined.

I undid my harness and drew my feet up underneath me. Carefully, I pushed myself up so I was standing in the cockpit. The Po-2 shifted sideways slightly, almost making me fall. I grabbed a hold of one of the struts and swung a leg over the side. I didn't have a problem with heights or jumping out of planes, but plunging to my death was not in my plan.

The freezing wind whipped my coat around me like a flag, rippling and tugging, threatening to drag me over the side. Again, I swallowed hard, and licked my lips.

"Keep it still," I called into the bitter wind, hoping she could hear me. I swung my other leg over. Maybe a rope, next time, so if I fell, Antonina could haul me back in.

"I'm trying to," she yelled back. I felt the plane slow, to almost stalling speed and reminded myself to thank her later.

"Focus," I muttered trying to calm myself. I lowered myself down, so I was crouching on the lower wing of the biplane, my hand firmly gripping the strut. Taking a breath, I leaned forward and nudged the bomb rack with my fist. It had ice around it, just enough to make the release mechanism stiff. It was all too common a problem in these bitter winters. The Po-2 wasn't designed for this; the whole setup was makeshift at best.

My hair whipped across my face. I couldn't spare a hand to brush it off, so I had to turn my face enough to let it blow clear. I caught sight of lights, far beneath my feet. We rushed toward them so quickly I felt giddy. I had to force my eyes up, away from the ground and concentrate.

I leaned down a little more, grabbed the side of the bomb rack and shook it, hoping the momentum wouldn't make me fall over the side. With a subtle crack as ice broke away and a forlorn creak, it opened and the bombs fell free. Feeling a little nauseated, I watched their silent descent. They were quickly swallowed by the darkness. I fancied I could hear a rushing sound as they fell, but I think it might just have been the blood pulsing through my ears.

I didn't wait to watch them explode. With the wind forcing me over the side, I rose quickly. I threw myself headfirst back into the cockpit, breathing heavily. My legs quickly followed and I lay panting, my head spinning with the sheer insanity of what I'd just done. I shut my eyes and savoured the feel of aircraft beneath and around me. I was very happy to still be alive.

It took at least a couple of minutes for me catch my breath and wriggle back into a sitting position. The sound of my harness clicking back in was particularly gratifying.

"That was so great," Antonina called out. "Do it again."

"Not a chance!" I called back. "You do it next time."

I heard her laugh and picked up a pencil to throw at the back of her head. I missed; my hands were shaking too badly from the rush of fear and adrenaline. I laughed as well, but it sounded a little bit hysterical in my own ears. My mouth clamped shut to cut off the sound.

I felt the plane bank and head back to the base. I closed my eyes and let myself relax for a little while. We'd soon land, refuel, rearm and be back up in the sky, but for a few minutes I could enjoy the ride. All I could hear and feel was the wind, the popping of the engine, the plane around me and the cold of my cheeks. I almost forgot there was a war on, until I felt our altitude drop as we came in to land.

Small lights showed Antonina where the runway was. She steered it and landed perfectly between the lights, not bumping the landing unnecessarily. She always flew with economy, if not with flair. There were enough showy pilots amongst us; it was nice to be paired with a conservative one. I don't want to suggest she lacked courage or the ability to get us out of a tight spot, because she didn't. She merely didn't feel the need to show off. Even if I didn't have to, I'd still trust her with my life.

The aircraft taxied off the runway, making way for the next pair to land, and headed down to where Sophia and Valentina were waiting, just off to one side. Sometimes I wondered how they felt, having to wait for us. It was never long, usually only about fifteen minutes, but that might feel like a lifetime on a cold, dark night. I decided I would have to ask them later if they sang or danced to pass the time.

The moment the plane stopped, Antonina hopped out and started gushing.

"You should have seen her, it was incredible. The bombs got stuck and she just climbed out onto the wing like an acrobat and pushed them out." Her hands gestured wildly, although she could barely be seen in the pale light. It didn't matter, her enthusiasm more than made up for it.

Luckily for me, it was too dark for anyone to see me blushing as I climbed out of the plane. Did she really have to mention it at all? I was simply doing my job, the same as everyone else. I had hoped to quietly mention it to our commander and hope she could come up with a solution. Maybe a rope from the cockpit to the bottom of the bomb racks which could be used to tug at them? Or...

"It was nothing, really," I muttered. "I was..." I had the sudden sensation no one was listening, which was fine, because I hadn't wanted to make a fuss anyway. I started to turn away, only to realise they were intent on something else. In the faint light from the runway, I could see their faces, looking behind the plane, toward the landing strip.

"They're a little low, aren't they?" Antonina asked, sounding concerned.

Frowning, I turned around and looked. She was right. The plane coming in just behind us was far too low. We could vaguely hear the tell-tale pop-pop of their engine. It hadn't stalled and wasn't struggling. Everything about the approach seemed right, except for the altitude. That and the fact that a plane was just taking off. It would reach the same altitude within seconds.

The second Po-2 lifted off, barely more than a shadow, even though the clouds had parted to allow in a sliver of moonlight.

"I don't think they can see each other..." Valentina's voice was high and wavered fearfully.

"Oh no..." I whispered. I drew my lower lip in between my teeth, bit down hard and hoped with everything I had that they'd pass by each other. Senior Lieutenant Bershankskaia and Major Rakova were going to punish the incoming pilot for making such a dangerous mistake.

I had just finished that thought when the sky was ripped apart.

CHAPTER 11

Someone screamed. The sound was high and raw, full of pure horror. I don't know where the scream had come from, but it haunted my dreams for years afterward. I have never heard such a sound, before or since, that perfectly captured my emotions but made me want to cover my ears and block it out.

One of the aircraft started banking and gaining altitude, but it was too little and too late. As I held my breath, time stood still. The wind fell silent. The only sound I was aware of was the rushing of blood into my ears. My heart pounded and I felt so helpless. All I could do was watch.

The two Po-2s collided.

Time resumed. The air was filled with the sickening sound of tearing canvas and splintering wood. I could hear the screams of my sisters in the air. They couldn't bail out. Even if they had parachutes, they were too low. They would never have opened in time.

I winced at the sickening crunch as one plane tore the wing from the other. They separated, a mess of damaged aircraft. For a moment, they seemed suspended in the air, like a grotesque mobile hanging over a baby's crib.

Something caught alight in one of the Po-2s, probably a fuel tank. In the next moment, it was engulfed in flames.

The wood and canvas caught alight like paper, incinerating the plane and its occupants before I could draw another breath. They had been the outgoing plane, I realized with horror.

I threw a hand over my eyes to shield them from the light and heat of the inferno; and any debris that might have been flung ground ward.

The second aircraft was caught in the explosion and tossed like a wooden toy. What control the pilot had was lost. The plane fell into a dive. It seemed to fall in slow motion, moving in time to the deafening roar of blood through my ears, before it slammed into the ground.

An eerie silence fell, during which everyone was frozen on the spot. No one made a sound; I wasn't sure my heart even beat. Then the moment passed and the field became a hub of activity and dismay.

There wasn't a single person on the field that night, man or woman, who didn't run straight toward the crashed plane. There were no bombs on board, parts of the Po-2 were still intact; there was still a chance someone had survived.

Through a haze of tears, I saw Evdokiia Bershankskaia and Major Raskova running ahead of me. I pulled up as a huge crowd gathered around the fallen plane, torches in hand, worried and scared faces gathered together.

It was one of the male trainers, a tall, thin, stern man named Kovalenko, who had spoken out against us girls in our earlier months, who reached the plane first. None of us much liked him, but he was extremely good at his job. Fearlessly, he scrambled over the wreckage, his long limbs moving him quickly on to the front cockpit where the pilot lay slumped forward.

He touched her, his thin fingers pressed against her neck. He scowled and stood perfectly still for what seemed like hours. It must really have only been a minute, if that.

I heard him curse under his breath and blushed slightly at hearing such explicit language. How silly I felt for worrying about that at a time like this.

Kovalenko scrambled over to the navigator and felt for her pulse as well.

When he looked up to address the crowd, my heart sank.

"Both dead," he declared harshly. "Waste. Nothing but waste." He jumped down from the wreckage and started away from it. "Foolish women," he snarled as he stalked past Major Raskova.

She watched him walk away, her mouth tight with well-controlled anger. Did he think she didn't feel the loss the most acutely of us all?

I started to cry, just a little at first. Then all of the girls around me were crying as well. Someone grabbed me and I found myself in an embrace with the rest of my crew.

"Who...?" Valentina asked the question we'd all be wondering, or I had at least.

"Anna Averin and Mariya Golova," Sophia replied. The two women who had spoken out against the Po-2 not an hour earlier. "And Evgenia Derova and Darya Blokhin."

I glanced skyward, past Sophia's head. Bits of burning plane were still falling, glowing embers like red snow on the breeze. There was no chance of either the pilot or her navigator having survived the inferno. I could only hope they hadn't suffered too much.

"Four girls," Valentina sobbed, leaning against us for support. "Four girls dead, and we haven't even gone to the front yet."

"If we do at all now," Antonina said softly. She wiped tears from her eyes with the sleeve of her coat. "They might think we're not capable, after this."

"But surely they wouldn't…" I started.

"Antonina is right," Sophia interrupted. She sniffed loudly. She never did anything by half. "If they're looking for an excuse not to send us, or to keep us here for longer, this will be it."

I felt sorry for myself, until I stopped to think about the women's loved ones. "Poor Major Raskova, she'll have to write to their families…" She would do it too, I had no doubt. She could have left it to her chief of staff, Militsa Kazarinova, but she would take the loss of four women personally. She'd probably handwrite four different letters of condolence.

"Yes. I don't envy her…" Sophia agreed.

"Ladies." Major Raskova's voice broke across the sobs and low voices of those gathered. "Drills are cancelled for the night. Get some sleep."

"Who will sleep?" Antonina whispered.

Silently, I agreed, fully.

*****

I lay awake for a long time afterward. No one had wanted to leave the airfield until Anna and Mariya's bodies were removed from the wreckage. Some of the male pilots had helped to carry them into a cool room, where they were laid carefully on tables. Tomorrow, they'd be buried and we'd officially mourn them. A hunt would be conducted for any remains from Darya and Evgenia.

In the meantime, mechanics and armourers set to work on clearing away the shattered body of the aircraft, scrounging for spare parts. We watched them for a while, before our commanders sent us away to our beds.

Sophia was snoring in minutes. I envied her ability to sleep so easily. Not long after, I lay listening to the rhythmic breathing of Valentina and Antonina. They both muttered in their sleep. Maybe the horrors of what they'd seen invaded their dreams.

I rolled over and back. I closed my eyes; I stared at the ceiling; I counted sheep. Nothing would help me to sleep.

In the very back of my consciousness, I gradually became aware of a sound.

It was distant, but very definitely the sound of piano music. Who would be playing in the middle of the night?

Curious, I gave up trying to sleep and got up. I slept in socks, we all did, so I pushed my feet into my boots, which mercifully now fit, and wrapped my coat around myself. I smiled, remembering Sophia putting her coat on over her nightgown and getting caught for it.

As quietly as I could, I slipped out of the room and down the corridor. It was incredibly difficult to be silent on the hard floors, so I walked, heel then toes, to reduce the sound of my footsteps as best I could. I would not want to wake one of the girls from her much needed sleep.

I made my way down the corridor toward the music and stopped outside a small room at the back of the building. What its original use might be, I could only guess at, but it had been long ago commandeered by us.

The door was ajar, so I peeked inside. There, sitting at a small, upright piano, which was hard up against the right hand wall, was Major Raskova. She looked so intent on her playing, that I simply stood and listened, entranced by the sound, like one of the Pied Piper's lost children.

She stopped playing and I realised I was probably intruding on a very private moment. I turned to step away, before she saw me, but she spoke before I'd moved more than a step.

"You couldn't sleep either?"

I looked back inside, guilty and blushing.

"I'm sorry ma'am, I didn't mean to—."

"No, please come in, sit." She patted the bench beside her.

Obediently, I walked in and slipped onto the seat beside her.

"Do you play?" She fingered one of the ivory keys, which had yellowed with age.

"No ma'am," I replied, "but I like to listen." I knew she had been an accomplished musician and, as a child, had wanted to be an opera singer. I'd heard her singing on the train, when everyone had been singing together, all of Raskova's women, and Raskova herself. She had a lovely voice and I'm sure it would have been celebrated all over the world.

She played something soft and sweet, and sad. Even just a few notes were almost enough to bring me to tears.

"It's been a difficult day," she said, playing a few lower, sadder notes.

"Yes ma'am," I agreed, speaking softly. "For us all."

"It's never nice to lose people." She turned to look at me, appraising something about me. "Is that why you can't sleep?"

"I think so, ma'am." I took a breath and plunged on. "And I'm worried. They say we might be sent home, because we're not fit to fly."

"Oh? Who says that?" She seemed bemused, rather than angry.

"Some of the other girls."

She took her hands from the piano and swivelled around to face me. "Have I said so?" Her tone was firm, but not unkind.

"No, ma'am," I conceded.

"Then why are you worried? Have I not worked hard to get you all here and trained in the first place?"

"Yes, of course you have." I wasn't sure where this was going.

"Well then, I'm hardly going to give up on us all now, and I'm not going to let anyone keep us from fighting." She looked so determined; I understood now how she always seemed to get her way. I felt my mouth turning up and tried not to grin at her passion.

"I see I'm amusing to you," she added teasingly. "Oh don't worry, I don't bite. And don't think we're going to be kicked off the base. However…" She held up a finger. "These are serious times and call for serious voices and serious faces." She turned back to the piano and played the silliest sounding tune I'd ever heard. It was full of fast, high notes and made me laugh.

"What else are you worried about?" she asked, slowing to a more sombre tune. "That you'll end up like Anna, Mariya, Darya and Evgenia?" She glanced over at me, but didn't stop playing. Her brow was creased slightly, her expression concerned but firm. "I told you when you volunteered that you may lose friends or die. You said you understood, did you not?"

"Yes ma'am," I replied, trying not to be meek in the face of her scrutiny. "But knowing it, being ready for and then to have it actually be real — I watched four of my friends die today. My sisters." My chest felt tight and I fought back the tears, but was betrayed by a sob that broke loose from between my lips.

Raskova stopped playing and put her arm around me. I leaned against her, hot tears sliding down my face. For a long while, she just let me cry. I thought I heard a sob or two from her as well, but she was in check much quicker than I was. I knew she'd lost friends already, most notably Osipenko, who had died only a year after their record-breaking flight in the Rodina.

Eventually, when I'd run out of tears, she spoke. "I can't promise it'll get any

66

easier," she said softly. "And I can't promise this won't be the last time. But I can promise you're strong enough to deal with it when it happens. I saw that in you on the day we met. You reminded me a little of me, when I was younger."

She smiled softly, reminding me with a start that she was only ten years older.

I sat up and wiped my sleeve across my eyes to dry them. "Of you?" How could I possibly be anything like her?

"Yes," she said. "Of me. We're both tough and we'll both do whatever it takes to do what needs to be done." She smiled in such a way that I knew she was remembering the cabbage incident. I blushed.

"We're survivors, you and I. Life can throw things at us and we'll get through them. Because we're determined not to let anything stand in our way and we don't let other people push us around. If we have to stand and fight, we'll do it, to our last breath. And that's why we'll be victorious. There is no other choice but success."

CHAPTER 12

"It's so unfair," Sophia whispered loudly.

I agreed with her, but I wisely kept silent on the matter, at least in public. I shifted from foot to foot, then forced my legs to keep still. I couldn't keep from blinking my eyes in the bright sunshine; they were watering from the glare. Or maybe it was bittersweet tears at another farewell, so close behind the last one.

I watched enviously as a beaming Lillya Litviak climbed into the cockpit of her brand new Yak-1. The Yakovlev aircraft had just been shipped from the factory and made our rickety Po-2s look little better than a flying lawn mower. A defenceless, slow, plodding, if reliable, lawnmower.

"We were supposed to go to the front first," Sophia continued her unsubtle rant. I could hear her breathing through her nose as though she were a dragon, ready to breathe fire. I didn't blame her, but she should save her ire for our sleeping quarters.

"Shhh!" In front of us, Lena had turned her head to urge her Sophia to silence, although I knew the pilot was as disappointed as the rest of the 588th regiment. We had been slated to go to the front first, but the accident with the two planes had forced a delay. We had to remain at Engels and train and drill for even longer, to appease those further up the chain of command. While we chafed to get out there, we understood the need to ensure no one died needlessly again. We were drilled endlessly in landing and cruising at the correct altitude until we were dreaming at the right height.

The funerals of the four girls had been harrowing. Four graves, all lined up, side by side, marked their resting places. We had all dressed in full uniform and turned out to hear Major Raskova and Evdokiia Bershankskaia say a few kind words about our friends; their friends, too.

They'd spoken of their bravery and persistence, their desires to defend the homeland they loved. They talked about individual traits each woman had displayed, such as Mariya's great love of dancing, and Anna's passion for intricate embroidery, which we never understood how she had time for. They talked about Darya's pretty singing voice and how Evgenia had hidden behind the gym to throw snowballs at the other women in winter.

They talked about details I'd known about, but I hadn't realised our commanding officers had. They noticed a lot more about us than I'd suspected. It made the funeral so much more personal and heartrending. No one had been able to keep from crying, then or for hours afterward.

Buoyed as I had been by my talk with Raskova in the piano room, I still cried. Even Lena Turova cried, although I had seen her bite the inside of her cheek so she wouldn't. She had been friends, of sorts, with both of the pilots. They had shared their train carriage all the way to Engels and had shared a room in the dormitory. She'd sat with them in the mess hall, even if they didn't laugh and joke with her, as they had with the others. She was too reserved and standoffish for that.

Most of the base had turned out for the funeral, but many of the male trainees had been bawled out by their trainers for wasting time.

"Women shouldn't be here anyway," Major Kovalenko had snapped, earning him a filthy look from every one of us. We didn't dare to speak out and Major Raskova was too polite to do it in front of us, but not one of us were either pleased or cowed by his attitude. She had been right in that respect, I wasn't going to let people like him stop me from fighting.

There was nothing any of us could do to stop people like him from delaying us though. I snapped back to the present at the sound of aircraft powering up. Their propellers were spinning until they became a blur, readying for their journey to the front. The thrum of the Yak-1's engine was like a purring cat.

They were fast, nimble and considerably stronger than the Po-2, which we now knew, was very fragile and highly flammable.

The 586th would need planes like this, I reasoned to myself, for fighting Germans. Our job, as night bombers, would be to hassle the enemy, like a flock of mosquitoes or flies. I tried to think of a nicer metaphor, one that didn't involve insects, but I couldn't. The point was, we didn't really need fighter aircraft. That didn't stop a little bubble of jealousy from forming in my chest, though. They were going to the front; today.

Lillya gave us a wave and we all waved back, decorum forgotten for a few moments, but with some measure of restraint. A few months ago, we would have run behind her plane until it lifted off the ground. She taxied her aircraft away from us and toward the runway, following her commanding officer in her own Yak-1.

I glanced sideways in time to see Major Raskova watching the regiment's ascent proudly. The woman had tears in her eyes; I could see them shining in the sun. She glanced at me and smiled, before turning back to the disappearing aircraft. Of course she'd be proud. She must have felt like a mother bird watching her chicks leave the nest, and hoping they'd some day return, or at least survive.

We watched until they'd disappeared over the horizon and the thrum of their engines had faded. The light breeze and the sound of trainee's planes took their place.

It was so peaceful that I was loath to leave, but Bershankskaia nodded her dismissal and walked away herself.

"Breakfast," Sophia declared. "I'm starving."

"You're always starving," Antonina pointed out.

"Yes I am," Sophia said cheerfully. "Let's go."

We headed to the mess hall, my stomach not particularly looking forward to the same old food. It was certainly better than nothing and a vast improvement on the bread and herring we'd had on the train, but it had long since become monotonous. A person could only eat porridge so often before it stuck in the throat.

The mess hall was bustling, as usual, but the loss of a couple of hundred women was going to make it considerably quieter. I glanced over to the tables the 586th used to occupy. The tables would be set for others now, probably for men, newly arrived to train to fight.

The four places at our table where the four women who had died remained unoccupied, but there was no longer a place set for them. For several days, empty plates and cups and clean cutlery had been left out for them, even though we knew they weren't returning. In spite of the strange or derisive looks the men gave us, we left them like that, as though a piece of those women still lived on. It helped us to grieve until we were ready to pack up the dishes and accept they were dead.

I slid into my place and looked down at the pile of mail someone had left on our table. I didn't bother to go through them, knowing none would be for me, and so was surprised then, when Sophia tossed one down beside my plate

"That's for you." She sounded as surprised as I felt. I grabbed it up and opened it quickly, tearing the back of the paper envelope.

The sheet of paper inside was neatly folded, its edges touching perfectly. Who did I know who was so precise? Perhaps this was the letter to inform me of my mother's death.

I glanced up at Sophia. She gave me a nod. "Go on, open it."

My hands were trembling. Strangely I was more scared of unfurling that page than I had been of standing on the wing of a plane in flight, trying to free the bombs.

I scanned the name at the bottom of the page. My heart skipped a beat.

"It's from Nikolai." To be honest, I'd started to think he'd forgotten me. So many months had passed since that time on the train when I'd gazed into those brown eyes…

I skipped back to the top and started reading.

My Dear Nadia,

I'm so sorry I haven't written sooner. Life at the front has left me little time to scratch my head, much less pick up a pen and write. There is so much to say, I'll try to remember it all. My regiment has been helping in the skies over Stalingrad. I'm sorry to say things have been bleak here. It seems like the front line changes daily, always back, always against us. We might push them back a few steps during the day, but it seems as though we're twice as many steps back by nightfall.

The Germans faired badly over the winter, though. I hope that knowledge cheers you as it cheered us. They invaded in their summer uniforms, which weren't warm enough for the winter. I think they're still finding bodies, frozen to death by the snow. Occasionally people appear and you see them in German boots. You don't ask how they came by them, but I know they've pulled them off bodies they found. It's gruesome, but the bodies no longer need them, so I try not to think about it too much.

Mostly, I think about you, and when you and your friends will get to the front. I remember how hard we all worked in training and believe me, you'll be glad for every second of it out here. You'll wish you had more training, but there's no time for more. Out here, you learn whatever you don't know. You learn it fast or you die.

I'm sorry. I shouldn't write things like that to you, but almost daily the people around me die. Soon, I started to think of death as normal. I didn't want to think like that, but everyone does. I want to think about that day on the train; how you looked and the scent of you. Sometimes, I want to run back to Engels, find you and run away somewhere we can be together. But I don't. I know neither of us will rest until every German is dead or gone from our homeland. Thinking of you makes even the longest days more tolerable.

I must go; I have another mission to fly. Another and another and another until we can meet again.

Stay safe,

Love, Kolya.

"Oh, love Kolya?" I hadn't noticed Sophia reading over my shoulder until she spoke.

I blushed.

"He sounds so troubled," I said sadly, folding the letter over. "Are we going to start thinking of death as normal?" I didn't want to imagine I'd see enough death not to be bothered by it any longer. How could any of the girls in my regiment die and not tear a hole in our hearts?

"No," Sophia replied firmly. "We're women. It's in our nature to be upset when people die. Men have colder hearts than we do."

I wasn't sure I agreed with her, but I nodded anyway. In spite of his assurances, I doubted Nikolai didn't feel every death as acutely as I would. Almost daily? That sounded as though he were surrounded by death, day and night. But of course he was; this was war.

I looked up at Sophia. "I miss Lillya," I sighed. I had no idea how long it'd be until I saw her again, but she'd have had some comment to cheer us all up. Maybe she'd have climbed into a cockpit and done barrel rolls a handspan off the ground and then look apologetic, as if she'd simply forgotten she wasn't supposed to do them.

It was going to be very quiet around here without the whole 586th regiment.

CHAPTER 13

In the end, our regiment was only delayed a month. Whether we were needed or they decided we were finally ready, they told us to pack our things and be ready to go to the front.

It was a sunny day in May, the day we were due to leave. I couldn't keep myself from smiling and neither could any of the other girls. We kept catching each other's eyes and grinning. Almost every time I opened my mouth to speak, someone else spoke at the same time and no one could finish her sentence because we laughed so much. We joked and teased and danced while we tidied our dormitory rooms. We sang loudly while we packed our suitcases.

Sophia laughed at the summer dress I had in my old suitcase along with my uniform. It was one I'd brought from home, when my mother wasn't looking, but I hadn't had time to wear it since leaving Moscow.

"Are you hoping to go to a dance at the front?" she teased. I stuck my tongue out at her and went on packing. I knew some of the girls had made sure to pack lipstick in their bags, so surely a dress was all right. Besides, even if I didn't wear it, it wouldn't hurt to remember we were still just young women at heart.

I closed up my suitcase, sadly remembering my mother doing that for me so long ago. Had she got the letters I'd sent her? I had no way to know, unless she replied.

I took a long, last look around at the dormitory room, the scruffy walls and worn floors; my home for the last seven months. Unless someone decided to delay us even longer, the chances were good I'd never be back here again.

"Are you going to miss it?" Valentina asked, raising an eyebrow at me.

"Of course not," I laughed. "I'm glad to leave. It's time we got to do some real work." Not that all the training hadn't been important and hard work. It certainly had, but I'd volunteered not to sit in a classroom but to fight the enemy.

Together, our crew and our regiment walked out to the parade grounds and turned out, our bags at our feet. I just wanted to get going, but our superior officers had decided to make a fuss, so we'd have to stand patiently and wait.

The garrison commander himself, Colonel Bagaev, stood before us — his uniform pristine, medals pinned proudly to his burly chest — and gave a little speech. His voice was deep and loud enough for us all to clearly hear, without having to strain.

"Today, for the first time," he began, "a women's regiment leaves our airfield for the front. You do not fly in awesome machines, but in training aircraft. And it's true; you yourself are not excessively awesome in appearance. But I am certain that in these light-winged airplanes, you will be able to inflict heavy blows on the enemy. Let fly with you, my fatherly wish: success to you and combat glory."

"Not awesome in appearance, hmmm?" I heard Antonina mutter, obviously slightly affronted by the comment. I glanced over at her, but she merely shrugged and grinned. At least we all agreed they weren't awesome machines. And no one could argue with his 'fatherly wish'; success against the enemy was something we all craved. I was less concerned with personal glory, but glory for my homeland was something I desired very much — glory and victory.

Colonel Bagaev dismissed us and nodded us toward the airfield. I didn't need to be ordered twice. I picked up my suitcase and headed toward the hardstand to which our Po-2 was tethered.

"Lillya would have been furious," Valentina commented, grinning about something. She lowered her bag to the ground and started untethering the aircraft.

"What? Why?" I looked at her in confusion.

"He said we're the first women's regiment to be sent to the front," she pointed out, wiggling her neatly shaped eyebrows at me.

I gaped at her until her meaning sunk in. The 586th had gone a whole month before us. Some of them would be mortified at such a slight, intended or otherwise.

I burst out laughing. "You're right. They'd all have been cranky to hear that."

"I dare you to write and tell her," Valentina said jokingly. At least, I thought she was joking.

"No way." I swung my case over into the cockpit and pushed it to one side. Four of us in one plane was going to be a tight fit, but we'd manage. By all accounts, we'd have to get used to it, too. At least I had Valentina in mine for this first flight. She was much smaller than Sophia. And I got to sit in front of her, so I could see and navigate without having her weigh me down.

If only we didn't have to fit our bags in as well. Even though they were small and packed as minimally as we could manage, they still took up space we weren't used to having occupied. Once Valentina was in and I climbed in too, we made ourselves as small as we could possibly manage.

"At least I'm not a man," the mechanic whispered teasingly in my ear. I blushed at the thought of being this close to anyone.

"I'll just pretend you're Kolya." That was the first time I'd used the diminutive version of Nikolai's name, but it felt good. Slightly less good was the sock Valentina gave me on my arm.

"Ow!" I exclaimed. Playfully, I leaned back, pressing her hard against the back of the cockpit.

"All right, I surrender." She laughed. "I can't breathe."

I sat forward again and twisted my upper body around to grin at her.

"I could tickle you, you know," she retorted.

"I could get us lost and end up flying away from the war," I threatened back.

"Now, now children!" Antonina called from the front cockpit, "don't make me come back there." We all laughed, like silly children, full of high spirits, off to a huge adventure.

I looked out of the cockpit and saw the 587th regiment. They'd turned out to watch us leave, just as we had when the 586th had left. I could just about feel their envy, but I knew they'd not be far behind. Major Raskova would, however, be accompanying us on our two-day journey to Morozovskaia. Having her leading us made me feel immensely proud and determined we'd do nothing to let her down.

*****

The whole regiment circled over Engels Air Force base, getting into formation before heading south-west. I could make out the old gymnasium and wondered if it'd be returned to its former use when all of the girls were gone. Maybe they'd make more women's regiments instead, although I suspected that was unlikely. With Major Raskova going to the front soon herself, there probably wouldn't be anyone to champion any other women. Time would tell.

The aircraft banked smoothly, straightened out and followed Raskova's Po-2 at a safe distance. All around me, I could hear the pop of engines and the roar of the late spring wind as it rushed past my ears. It was a perfect day for flying; nothing but us, the birds and a few low-lying clouds occupying the sky. It would have been perfect if I wasn't jammed so tightly into my cockpit, but even that didn't quash my enjoyment too much.

Halfway to Morozovskaia, we landed at a small field near a tiny village, about an hour before the sun set. We'd stop here for the night to rest, refuel and, mercifully, relieve our bladders. We had no tubes or bottles for that, as the men did, so we had to hang on and avoid drinking too many liquids. Even during drills, we'd have to run off while the mechanics and armourers were working to relieve ourselves. A full bladder at high altitudes wasn't pleasant.

The entire village turned out to stare at us.

"Female aviators, had anyone heard of such a thing before?" Antonina whispered, raising her eyebrows and glancing over in Raskova's direction.

"Not so many and not so pretty," Valentina replied. "Oh, is that fresh bread?" It was. We ate well that night, although we made sure not to eat excessively. Everyone was struggling to keep food in their bellies, without a regiment of hungry airwomen eating the village out of its rations.

They were good enough to let us billet in their cottages for the night as well, which included, oh joy of joys, a bath.

"I could get used to this," I sighed, curling up on a rug on the floor, under a thin blanket, revelling in cleanliness.

"You're getting spoilt," Antonina teased. That didn't stop her from stretching languidly like a cat and closing her eyes.

"It's a palace, after the gymnasium," Sophia pointed out, yawning.

I murmured my agreement and closed my eyes. I wasn't used to sleeping at night any longer, but for a few hours I got some rest, before lying awake, listening to the sounds of the night, until dawn came to rouse us all.

We ate a quick breakfast and took off into a day that was a carbon copy of the one before. The tailwind was light, the clouds were few. The sun shone over us, arching up before us gradually as the hours passed.

About ten minutes from our destination, Antonina let out a sudden cry and pointed out over our left wing. A little bit fearfully, I followed her gesture with my eyes and saw a fighter plane appear from out of the increased cloud cover. Then another, and another. They flew past our regiment, soaring by us on our left. I watched them bank, in perfect formation before coming back around.

I thought they were heading right for us, but instead they roared over our heads, so close their engines made our aircraft shudder as the airstream was interrupted briefly.

My heart had started to thud at the sight of them, immediately assuming the worst. The Germans had come to kill us, in our defenceless aircraft, before we really even reached the front. I had known I might die, but not like this, not without dropping a single bomb onto the enemy.

I wished I had a grenade to toss at them, until I squinted into the sunshine and looked more closely at them. I groaned aloud when I spied the red star painted on the wings of the closest fighter.

"They're ours." I watched them circle back and buzz us again, this time parting their formation in the centre and flying around us. They flew so fast, it was like watching eagles circling a flock of chickens. The sight was so magnificent, I couldn't help the surge of pride and patriotism in my chest.

"Where are they going?" Antonina called through the intercom.

"Who?" I called back, but Valentina tapped my shoulder and pointed out to the right. Some of our planes had dropped out of formation and scattered into the sky.

"Can't they see they're ours?" I exclaimed. "It's not like they're painted with swastikas."

"I don't know," Valentina replied, yelling into my ear. "They're going to be in trouble with our commander!"

I winced and nodded my agreement. Major Raskova was not going to be impressed with those pilots. Our escort fell back and I soon lost sight of them. I forgot them quickly enough, as Morozovskaia came into view in front of us and, back in proper formation, we descended to our first base at the front lines.

CHAPTER 14

The small village of Trud Gorniaka, near Morozovskaia, was to be our home until we were sent elsewhere. It was the sort of place I wouldn't have gone to, if not for its proximity to the front. It consisted of a few dozen cottages — each with their own small vegetable garden — two, perhaps three streets and a road. And now an aviation army base, however makeshift it might be. Aircraft and hardstands covered ground that might have been grassy, but was now well trodden and muddy.

The base was a bustle of activity when we touched down. Several aircraft took off and landed before and behind our formation. Mechanics and armourers hurried here and there, refueling and rearming their planes. Few stopped to pay much attention to the new arrivals. I wasn't sure what I'd pictured when I thought of the front, but it wasn't this, at least not yet. Perhaps I'd thought we'd see fighting, death and dying a mere ditch away from us. That wasn't the case. We were far enough back to protect us, or more importantly our planes, from discovery and destruction by the enemy.

Not, I was certain, that anyone here would rest easily or be complacent. The threat of attack was real and constant. The fear that this might some day be German territory was all too horribly real. I swallowed hard as the Po-2 trundled along on its fixed wheels. I wasn't going to let fear cripple me so I'd myself and my sisters down. We had worked hard to get here; we'd prevail.

Ground crews directed us to taxi off the landing strip, which was nothing more than a flat field, well worn from boots and wheels. Antonina followed their gestured directions and steered toward the hardstands to tether our aircraft. I had to sit forward, to let Valentina out first, since it'd be her job to ensure the Po-2 wasn't able to roll or fly off in a high wind. Losing a plane from something as silly as a badly tied tether would be disastrous and incredibly embarrassing.

The fighters who had served as our escort had already landed and their pilots stood near their aircraft, watching us approach. They were all men, of course. I hadn't expected otherwise. Many were young enough to be called boys; they barely looked old enough to shave. I envied them their aircraft, though. I doubt there were many regiments in the entire Air Force who didn't have better machines than ours.

The men were all smiling, which buoyed my spirits, albeit briefly.

I climbed out of the cockpit to a gale of male laughter. I thought nothing of it as I hauled my suitcase out of the cockpit and jumped down from the wing. I put my case down on the grass and went back for my maps. Only then did I realize the laughter hadn't let up.

Glancing over toward the men, I saw them mimicking planes in flight, their arms in the air to either side of them, hands out straight.

Boyish exuberance. I started to smile until three or four zoomed away from the others, heading in different directions, shrieking, "The Germans are coming to get us. Ohhhh, save us. Save us!" The rest of the men laughed as though the sight was the most hilarious thing they'd ever seen.

Even though I was standing on the lower wing, obscured by a strut, I glared at them. I didn't even need to look to know that the rest of my crew was doing the same thing. We hadn't left formation, and surely no one had insisted they fly so close to us. Even if they were on our side, their behavior might have endangered us.

If I thought they were terribly rude, so did most of the other girls. A couple even started to cry.

This only set the men off into more laughter. "Hey, you little girls, can you tell a star from a swastika?" They howled, doubled over with derisive mirth. "Maybe you should go home to your mothers. Or go back and train properly!"

"I'll give them little girls," Sophia growled, hauling her bag out of the cockpit as though she planned to club them with it. She twisted around and threw it so heavily it left an impression in the dirt and made a thump to match.

"Ignore them," Antonina said breezily, taking off her helmet. Her neat plaits were pinned in place to her head, but she was pretty and feminine enough to make the men stop laughing and look at her instead. She turned to look at them, but she ignored the wave a couple of them offered her.

"Those girls should have known better," Sophia had obviously decided to vent her anger on them instead. "They made us all look bad."

I glanced over to where Major Raskova stood beside two of the crying women, Anya and Klavdia. Her voice was too low to hear what she was saying, but I could tell she wasn't pleased. She was frowning and gesturing subtly up toward the sky, in the direction from which we'd come. I could only assume she'd heard the men laughing and was furious any of us had given them a reason.

Raskova reached out to touch Klavdia's arm in a reassuring gesture, but her expression was stern. I didn't need to hear to know that she was saying, 'You made a mistake, but never, ever, do it again.' I was glad not to be on the receiving end of her disappointment this time. I remembered the look she'd given me on the train and still wanted to wither at the memory. I had never felt so bad in my life. I almost felt sorry for the girls, but their actions could have had repercussions for us all.

"Do you think this will delay us again?" I asked, keeping my voice low enough for only my friends to hear. "I mean, something like this might make them think we're all not ready." Fancy mistaking Soviet planes for German ones. If they did that out at the front lines, it could get people killed. Leaving formation could make them an easy target for a lucky Messerschmitt. I swallowed. I wasn't looking forward to meeting German aircraft in the skies.

From the look of consternation on their faces, the other three were thinking the same thing. At the rate we were going, the war really would end before we saw any action. I shivered in the light breeze and picked up my suitcase.

"I suppose we'll just have to work hard to prove ourselves." If they'd only give us the chance to do that. I sighed and hefted my suitcase up higher. "Come on, let's get settled."

I glanced back to see Bershankskaia approaching Raskova and the two pilots, an uneasy feeling in my stomach. They had to let us fight. They just had to.

*****

We entered the village and were assigned to various cottages, the occupants of which had agreed to accommodate us during our short time in Trud Gorniaka. Our cottage, although small, was neat, with a tidy garden. The windows were surrounded by shutters, painted red, which looked well used. Doubtless they were closed nightly to prevent German planes from seeing any trace of light inside. This close to the front, even a small light could quickly mean death for anyone in the cottage or those in the cottages around them. No one wanted to give the enemy a handy target.

The tidy little home belonged to a woman named Olga, who looked as though she could wrestle half the German army and win without breaking a sweat. She wore her hair short, just curling at the nape of her neck. There wasn't more than a centimetre of fat anywhere on her, but she had the build of a carthorse, and a warm, generous smile.

Her front room, into which we were shown by helpful ground crew, was filled with all sorts of little nick-nacks. Babushka dolls painted in bright colours; wooden bowls full of colourful beads; bright woollen rugs covered the backs of chairs; and the worn timber floor. A shelf to one side of the room was filled with books, most of which seemed to be poetry.

In the centre of the room was a round and well-used table, covered in marks from many years of crockery and cutlery gracing its surface. One leg was supported by a book, to — I assumed — stop it from wobbling whenever it was used. A woven basket sat atop it, empty now, but it looked to have once held fruit, perhaps apples. Such things were luxuries now.

"Welcome." Olga embraced all four of us, one after the other. When it was my turn, her arms squashed me, making breathing a momentary challenge. It was nice though, to be greeted in such a maternal way. Up until now, Bershankskaia and Raskova had been like mothers to us, but at the age of thirty-one, I doubt either liked the idea of being a parent to girls as old as us.

"You're all welcome here, as long as you need, but no funny business with the men." She waggled a long finger at us, at the height of my nose, and looked firm. "I won't have girls like that here. Only respectable girls for Olgas. Especially you." She waggled her finger especially hard at Sophia. "Pretty girls like you, I won't have you getting into trouble."

I struggled to keep from laughing at the expression of surprise on Sophia's face. I wasn't sure anyone had ever called her pretty before, she certainly wouldn't have. She always considered herself far too masculine to be pretty. Personally, I'd always thought she was unkind to herself. She might not be the beauty Antonina and Lillya were, but she was sweet and a good friend.

"I have my eye on you all." Again she waved her finger.

Valentina went cross-eyed from watching it move back and forth. I had to bite the inside of my cheeks to keep a straight face.

"Yes Olga," we all replied meekly. She looked us over, as if suspecting insincerity. She really didn't have anything to worry about. The four of us were too busy and dedicated to have time for boys, unless that counted the occasional letter or rare moment of flirting in the mess hall. We certainly wouldn't be sneaking boys back to our rooms, or sneaking out at night for a secret rendezvous.

Especially the last, since our missions would all take place at night.

"Good girls, we'll get along well then. Go settle into your room. The window is nailed shut, so no boys can climb inside."

"Yes Olga, thank you Olga." We hurriedly retreated to the room we'd been assigned, at the back of the cottage.

"Oh my, the woman would scare Major Raskova," Valentina giggled, trying to keep her voice down.

"She'd scare the German army," Antonina replied, her blue eyes huge. "Maybe we should take her up with us."

I put my hand over my mouth to muffle my laughter. "You girls are terrible," I giggled.

"I think Olga is all right," Sophia said lightly. She put her bag down on a bed near the window and turned to face us. "I think she has very discerning taste." My friend still wore the same surprised expression she had out in the front room.

Valentina, who had opened her bag, grabbed out a pair of socks and threw them at Sophia. "Of course you would think that."

"What?" Sophia asked guilelessly.

"I'm watching you," Antonina wagged her finger under Sophia's nose. "No sneaking out for kissy-kissy under the trees with those nasty boys."

For a moment, the three of us just stared at her. Then we all fell about laughing.

CHAPTER 15

I barely slept that night. I wasn't sure I'd ever sleep at night again. I should have been used to the sound of planes coming and going, but it was different here. They were flying out to real targets. The shouts from the ground crews seemed more urgent, the engines sounded louder. Even Sophia's robust snoring sounded different.

When the sun finally peeked through a gap in the shutters, I was almost ready to sleep. I pushed the blanket off me and went to shake the other girls awake. Rousing Sophia was always risky; she was as likely to wake up swinging her arms as she was to simply open her eyes.

Luckily, this morning she just woke and minutes later we were pressing our feet into our boots and straightening our shirts. I honestly had no idea what to expect of the coming day. The military didn't tend to share its plans with people like me, especially when the front line was such a fluid, changeable thing. Even if they did include us in decision-making, the next day things might have changed.

We headed out for breakfast in the mess, which consisted of tables set up under a tall tree. I assumed on rainy days, we'd cram into the small kitchen, or our billets, or sit under aircraft wings to eat.

We ate quickly, knowing Major Raskova was returning to Engels this morning. I doubt anyone wanted to miss saying goodbye. I knew I didn't. Hopefully her departure would be more successful than our arrival.

I glanced around. Anya and Klavdia were sitting together, with Katya and a pilot named Irina, who was Evdokiia Bershankskaia's chief of staff. Irina had stayed in formation, of course. The other three looked sombre. Anya's eyes were red and looked as though she hadn't slept last night either.

Directly after breakfast, Raskova stood, silently demanding our instant attention.

"Ladies, please attend to your planes and be ready for an inspection by

Division Commander Popov." Her expression was calm, even as her eyes flickered over to where those two pilots sat. I didn't need her to say more to understand her underlying message— 'Don't anyone mess up again.'

I swallowed hard and rose to my feet. None of us said a single word all the way to the plane. Even Sophia was quiet. We'd had a visit from General Vershinin, the leader of the 4th Air Army the previous afternoon, after we'd taken our bags to Olga's. I had gotten the impression he approved of us. He'd probably been the one to assign us to the 218th Night Bomber Division, under Popov, in the first place.

I'd liked General Vershinin. He had kind eyes and wrinkles around them like people got when they smiled a lot. He also looked tired and weighed down by responsibility. That he had a high opinion of Major Raskova was obvious and that heightened mine of him.

He'd looked over our aircraft and asked Raskova questions about our training. He looked at us with interest and respect, which I wasn't accustomed to when it came to male officers. Some of the girls even giggled over him, out of his hearing of course, which I thought was silly. He seemed sweet, but he was so old compared to us.

We clambered all over the plane that morning, checking the engine, looking over the wings, making sure the bomb racks were in place. I sat under a wing and looked over the maps, while Sophia crouched down under the plane. The bombs she held balanced on her knees were heavier now. I felt bad for not helping, but I wouldn't be helping her while on missions and she always said she didn't mind the work.

Everything was in perfect operational order when Bershankskaia shouted for us to stand beside our aircraft. It only took us moments to be standing at attention; backs straight, eyes straight, ready for inspection. It was so different from that night when the girls had worn coats over their nightgowns that I had to force myself not to smile.

The desire for anything close to amusement evaporated the moment I set eyes on Alexei Popov. He was a tall man, lean and strong, with a receding hairline. His uniform was immaculate, as I would have expected of our Division Commander. He walked with great purpose from one Po-2 to another, looking over each plane, but barely glancing at the crews.

I understood that at this point in the war, we had more pilots than planes, so the receipt of a regiment of aircraft, even if they were only our little biplanes, was an important matter. I thought perhaps he was less concerned about who crewed them than the fact he had more planes to command.

I thought again when he stepped up to our plane. The look of utter distain in his blue-grey eyes made my blood run cold. Even after the teasing and derision we'd received from so many of the male pilots and trainers, I'd never before seen such open hostility. He clearly didn't want us here at all.

I swallowed hard and kept my eyes forward, hoping he wouldn't look straight at me. I couldn't be sure I wouldn't return his look of hostility with one of my own. I didn't have to worry; I doubt he even registered my existence beyond a glance at my maps, rolled neatly and stowed in a bag under the wing. I thought maybe I'd be chastised for leaving them there, but he didn't deign to address me at all before moving on.

I turned to watch him give Lena and her crew the same treatment. The pilot's face was turning pink in obvious ire at being ignored. If Popov noticed Lena's annoyance, he didn't comment or show any sign. For once, she and I were in complete agreement. Until, that is, she turned her dirty look on me once the commander had passed. I frowned at her, confused as to what she thought I'd done to warrant such a look. Her scowl deepened and she looked away.

Evidently finished inspecting our aircraft, Popov stood back and addressed us all. His voice was deep, commanding and loud enough to reach us all.

"You think you're ready to fight?" he challenged, his eyes traveling across the line of women. Assuming the question was rhetorical, no one responded. This only made him frown.

"All these little princesses I am sent," he went on. "Princesses who cannot stay in formation when under attack. Princesses who scream and cry when faced with friendly planes. Little girls who lack basic discipline."

I bit my lip and hoped Sophia would keep her mouth shut. From the corner of my eye I could see her becoming upset. Most of us hadn't cried and none had screamed. The male pilots had, but only when making fun of us. And not one of us would have thought of ourselves as a princess. Speaking out against Popov would get us arrested and thrown in the guardhouse, but that didn't mean we had to like what he was saying.

"I say," he went on, "that you are not ready to fly. You will undergo further training. You will train with Major Nechepurenko until I deem you fit to fight. If I deem you fit."

Now I wanted to cry. It was so unfair. We had done nothing wrong. We would, of course, do as we were ordered and we'd support Anya and Klavdia, who would doubtless blame themselves for this. They were still our sisters, even if they had made a mistake that caused us yet another delay.

I glanced at Sophia. She had her teeth clenched so hard her jaw was turning white.

"While the Germans advance, we wait," I heard her mutter. Although she was right, I hoped Popov didn't hear.

*****

Major Nechepurenko was a considerably more patient man than Popov, much to my relief. He was also the division navigator, so I looked to him to learn as much as I could about flying and combat.

He'd arrived just as Raskova was leaving, so he'd found many of us in tears. If he thought us princesses and lacking discipline, he was kind enough not to say so. He greeted us, instead, with great enthusiasm and stood with us to wave our beloved commander goodbye.

Immediately making himself a part of us, our regiment, was a very clever way to endear himself to us. Certainly, it was much more effective than a nasty upbraiding.

"Pilots and navigators, please, to your planes, in formation behind me." He gave us a chance to wipe our eyes and climb into our cockpits. Then we were skyward. With no radios in our aircraft, we had to watch closely and copy his every bank, ascent and descent.

"He's testing us," Antonina concluded, taking the Po-2 through a breathtaking series of manoeuvres. "This is fabulous!"

I had to agree with her. After all the training we'd done, this kind of flying was still something new.

"I envy you!" I called through the intercom.

I heard her laugh in reply. "Take the controls then!"

I looked at the ones in front of me covetously.

"Really?"

"Go ahead." I saw her hands rise above her head, to show she'd relinquished the plane to me. I hadn't flown in such a long time; it was a thrill to do it, even for a few minutes. I loved being in a plane, but being the one at the controls, making it soar and dip, there was nothing in the world that gave me a bigger thrill.

"We're coming in to land," Antonina pointed out, the landing strip laid out right in front of us. Sadly, I took my hands off the controls and sat back, my whole body buzzing from sheer adrenaline.

"Thank you!" I called out. I knew she'd understand the very great gift she'd given me and hoped we wouldn't get into trouble for it. I could take the punishment if we were; it was worth it.

We landed neatly behind our new trainer and jumped out. Far from being annoyed at the delay, we were all grinning at having had such an interesting flight. Even Lena Turova was smiling; a rare sight indeed.

Major Nechepurenko was smiling as well. "Now that I have some idea of what you do know, I know what you need to know." He frowned playfully at his own tongue twister. "Well, you understand what I mean. Come, they've been kind enough to set us up a classroom."

"Excuse me, sir," Katya asked boldly. "Do you think we're not ready?"

He looked down his long nose at her in surprise. "Oh, yes, well…young lady, uh, Private, I don't think anyone is entirely ready for combat unless they've actually done it and survived. And even then, perhaps we're not really ready to do it again. But I'll make sure you're as ready as we can get you. Come on now."

Which was no answer at all, to Katya's chagrin. Behind his back, she pulled a face, which I saw and had to stop myself from laughing. Perhaps Popov was right; we did lack discipline. However, I suspected Major Nechepurenko would have laughed had he seen it too. He seemed like the jovial sort, or maybe that was his way of coping with the war. Some people went to pieces in the face of hardship, while some turned tougher, so other people couldn't hurt or disappoint them. Still others became clowns. By being silly, it was easy to disguise your own emotions, even from yourself.

I resolved to try to be myself, no matter what I faced, but hardier folk than me had undoubtedly made the same resolution and had cracked under the pressure. I would be like Major Raskova, I decided, strong and tough, but still kind and openhearted. Flexible enough to bend when required, as far as necessary, without breaking.

CHAPTER 16

The second delay lasted for two weeks, but the pilots and navigators loved every minute of it. By the end, we all would have followed Major Nechepurenko anywhere. Well almost anywhere. Whether he had convinced Popov or if General Vershinin insisted we were ready, we flew our first real combat sortie in June 1942, a whole year after the fascists invaded, and nine months after I'd volunteered.

Our target was to be German encampments near the Mius River, where they'd dug in and were trying to push deeper into our motherland. Maybe later I'd be more curious about the strategic importance of each target we were ordered to bomb, but tonight I just wanted to be out there. Our first mission would be one I would never forget.

The engine of the Po-2 thrummed like a sewing machine. The constant popping of the five-cylinder engine competed with the rush of the wind. I adjusted my flight goggles for the thousandth time. They would probably never feel comfortable, since it was nerves and not the goggles that had me agitated.

I looked out at the other two Po-2s out in front of ours. Katya Aranova, Klavdia Nickova and their navigators were somewhere in the darkness, three minutes and six minutes respectively, ahead of Antonina and I. I couldn't see them, but their presence was reassuring nonetheless. How pilots went on solo missions, I couldn't imagine. Even with my sisters out there, my nerves were raw.

It was the perfect night for an attack, if there was a perfect night for such a thing. It was overcast, dark and cold. My nose and cheeks were numb from the frigid air rushing past the open cockpit. I wriggled my gloved fingers to make sure they were still awake.

Then, out of the darkness, a flare lit up the sky, falling slowly from one of my sister's aircraft. It was immediately met with red, white and green searchlights crisscrossing the sky. As with so many things, being told about them and actually seeing them were two entirely different things. For something that looked essentially benign they were terrifying. In those lights, the enemy might be able to spot us and know just where to aim to shoot us down. The thought of dying tonight made my mouth go dry.

A white searchlight flashed, briefly making Katya's Po-2 a black shadow against its brightness. My heart skipped a beat, but the light was gone from her a breath later. Evidently the Germans hadn't seen her. How long we would be so lucky was anyone's guess.

A sudden gust swept the Po-2 eastward a couple of metres, making my heart jump again. For a spilt second, I thought we'd been hit. Antonina turned the controls, just a hair, to adjust our heading. I drew in a deep breath. If I could just ignore the lights up ahead, and the beating of my heart, then maybe I could pretend this was just like a flight for fun, at night, in the dark. All I could hear was the thrum of the engine, the wind rushing past my helmet.

But I couldn't ignore my rapid heartbeat, the feel of sweat in my underarms, the adrenaline pulsing through my bloodstream. I was terrified, but I was excited. I'd waited for this night for so long.

I watched in fear as Klavdia's Po-2 flew right into the searchlights, before veering off east, drawing the fire of the anti-aircraft guns. Looking like tiny sparks of light, the tracer bullets fountained skyward, well clear of their marks. The Po-2 might be slow, but they could turn on a hairpin. The roar of gunfire was louder than I'd expected, but I felt strangely calm.

I watched as though through someone else's eyes as Katya's aircraft passed over the target. They must have dropped their bombs, because the ground exploded in a fiery rush, lighting up the sky for a couple of seconds. Everything went black and silent, but the searchlights were moving frantically, trying to pin us in their light.

Then it was our turn. I ignited a flare and dropped it over the side, showing Antonina exactly where to find the target. Keeping the aircraft low, she took us over the top of the small wooden huts where the Germans would have been trying to keep warm and get some much needed rest after the day of killing our countrymen.

"Not tonight boys," I heard Antonina laugh. She was actually enjoying this. Well, why not? We'd worked hard to do our bit and now we could.

Antonina turned off the engine letting the plane idle in the current of cold night air and glide across the encampment. The beauty of the Po-2, if there was one, was that it could fly this low, almost silently, our passing making little more than a whoosh, like a pair of witches on our armed, ancient broomstick.

Antonina placed a finger on the release button. I grabbed my torch from beside my on the seat and quickly shone it toward the wing. I only gave her long enough to check the paint mark on the wing where once we'd have used chalk, and switched off the light.

I heard her softly counting down, "Three, two, one…" She pressed the button and released the bombs. I couldn't see them fall, but the plane lifted slightly, lighter for the sudden loss of four hundred-kilogram bombs. I let out the breath I'd been holding and willed my heart to slow to a normal pace.

I felt Antonina switch the engine back on, and found myself holding my breath again as it sputtered back to life. A pull to the controls and a twist to the left and the little biplane sideslipped onto an easterly heading.

As we banked, the first of the bombs ignited and exploded, several feet from the nearest hut. Seconds later, Germans came pouring out of them, dressed in only their warm, long underwear, flames lighting them briefly for us to see. Antonina started laughing and I couldn't help but smile. It'd be comical if they weren't so furious. And armed.

We veered away, but the Germans were looking for us now, anti-aircraft shells and tracer bullets whizzed past, searchlights moving back and forth, systematically hunting. Another minute or two and we'd be clear. I held my breath again, resisting the reflex to close my eyes and keep them closed until we'd moved to a safe distance. With no small amount of willpower, I cracked them open, in time to see the red light of a tracer pass by my nose, so close I was sure they could see me. I ducked down further in the cockpit, all too aware it afforded little real protection.

Another shell hit the upper wing, leaving a small hole in the canvas, which did nothing to impede the Po-2's ability to fly. At least our first war wound wasn't in flesh.

The aircraft banked steeply, giving me a glimpse of a Po-2 coming in behind us, Lena Turiva's, I knew, with her navigator Inna. Thankfully the sweetest and most patient navigator had been more than happy to fly with Lena and keep her grounded (figuratively); they made a good team.

I didn't see their bombs, but I watched a hut explode, a sudden ball of fire in the night. It set fire to the ones to either side and soon several were burning, along with what looked to be a food supply store. Lena had found the target beautifully. I was happy for her. I'd have congratulated her later if I thought she'd care to hear. Maybe I'd try anyway.

Once we were clear, I was able to smile and privately declared our first mission to be a success. I closed my eyes for a few moments and let myself be lulled by the sound of the engine. We had damaged the enemy, we'd proved ourselves capable and I was incredibly pleased. Major Raskova would be proud. Popov might even be happy with us tonight. With a sigh, I switched on my torch and checked our bearings on the compass. It wouldn't do to succeed and then get lost on the way back.

Fifteen minutes later, we landed at the auxiliary field from which we were working all night. I threw down a flare to show Antonina where to land and she took us safely down. I quickly ran off behind a bush to relieve myself, as Sophia and Valentina attended to the plane. Five minutes later, we were refuelled, rearmed and headed back to the target.

*****

"You've done exceptionally well," Evdokiia Bershankskaia told us, standing at the front of the small briefing room back at Trud Gorniaka. I was exhausted, but buzzing with energy from the night's missions. Everyone had survived and our aircraft had only suffered minor damage; nothing that wouldn't be fixed in time for tonight. The thought of going back up filled me with a sense of dread, now that I knew what to expect. But we'd go, again and again, until we'd won.

Blinking, I focused on my regimental commander as she continued speaking. Concentrating while this tired was a challenge I'd conquered back at Engels, but it still battled with me, especially this morning. Honestly, I'd really hoped the briefing would be a chance to wind down, to help us sleep. I was quickly proven wrong.

"But there are some things we need to iron out." She looked around the room at us all. She looked tired too. Of course, she'd been at the auxiliary airfield all night as well, directing us and watching everyone closely. I didn't envy her job.

I groaned silently. What had we done wrong and would we need more training? I glanced at Sophia, who was clearly thinking the same thing. She smirked at me and shrugged.

"It's nothing bad." Bershankskaia laughed. She must have seen our exchange. I blushed.

"Firstly, I noticed every mechanic was very quick to attend to their planes when they came in. That is, of course, what you've been trained for and you did it admirably. However…" she paused for effect. I decided she must have been listening to too many of Raskova's speeches.

"Here it comes," Sophia muttered.

"I noticed when your planes weren't on the ground, you were standing around looking bored. It's Air Force regulations to have one pilot, one navigator, one mechanic and one armourer per plane."

It was, and it made no sense to me at all.

"However," she began again, "we'd be much more efficient if, when a plane arrived, everyone who was available could help out. Obviously, I expect you to see to your aircraft when it's grounded, but otherwise, work with the other crews. Armourers, two or three of you loading bombs would be much more efficient than one."

"Yes!" Sophia agreed loudly, earning a smile from our commander.

"And mechanics, one or two of you can be patching holes while another does the refuelling."

Valentina nodded vigorously at this.

"Further," Bershankskaia added, "we have just as many planes as pilots and just as many navigators and so on. I'd hate to think of losing any of you, but if we do, we'll have a very difficult gap to fill."

That was a depressing thought, but she was right. We didn't have a single woman who could be spared for death or even injury. Some pilots could fly without a navigator, but sooner or later we'd have to start grounding aircraft.

"With this in mind, I've asked for extra personnel, initially mechanics. The rest of you, I want the mechanics to train the armourers to fix and refuel the planes. Navigators," she glanced at me for a moment, "you'll be training the mechanics to navigate. And the navigators, those of you who can fly, will be practicing more and more, especially combat flying. We have the training aircraft; take turns flying to and from targets. I want everyone trained to do as many things as possible, so that if anyone is hurt, someone can step right into her place. The alternative," she added, smiling, "would be to recruit some men."

She grinned as we all shouted, "No! No way!" And, "No, no men!"

"I'm glad we all agree. Now get some sleep, you'll need it. We leave for the field an hour before sunset."

CHAPTER 17

My dearest Nikolai,

We've been at the front for a month now. To tell you the truth, I feel as though the days are starting to blur together. Or should I say the nights, since that is when we're on our missions. Sometimes I can't remember what time of day it is, what day of the week it is or even what month. I keep having to ask Antonina, who is keeping a diary of daily events. She says after the war, people will want to know all about us. I doubt they will, but of course I haven't said that to her. I think keeping a diary helps to get her through each day.

Every day is pretty much the same as the day before it. We fly to an auxiliary field, with Sophia and Valentina. You remember Sophia, don't you? She's my closest friend, but I feel squashed when she and I share a cockpit. I don't mind though, because we can chatter as Antonina flies. I can't tell you what we talk about, because it's girl talk and probably wouldn't interest you, but your name does come up here and there.

When we get to the other field (which has been carefully selected by one of our commanding officers, to make sure it's flat and not full of mines), we unload our things and receive our orders and target coordinates for the night.

Sometimes it's food stores, sometimes sleeping Germans, sometimes searchlights to make it easier for the other girls for the rest of the night; we do whatever is asked of us.

We share the field with a men's night bomber regiment. At first, they laughed at us and called us little girls, just like the boys at Engels used to. We ignored them of course, but we were determined to prove we were as good as they were. Because we work together, with the mechanics and armourers helping each other, our planes get back in the air faster than theirs. We keep up a continuous stream of planes, in a constant loop, three minutes apart, all night. This means we all fly ten to fifteen missions every night. The men fly close to eight. They counted once and stopped laughing after that.

I find it strange that they see how well we work but they don't copy us. Their mechanics spend half the night standing around, smoking cigarettes, talking about their rations of vodka and gossiping like ladies. In fact, we were told off for helping each other, but Evdokiia (Senior

Lieutenant Bershankskaia), said to keep doing what we're doing because it works, and that we weren't to worry about what anyone else says.

I was worried though, that she, and maybe the rest of us, might get arrested for breaking Air Force rules, but so far no one has said or done anything. Maybe eventually they'll see how well we're doing and follow our lead. Results are what matter, right? Anyway, Evdokiia is regimental commander, so we listen to her and keep working hard. Antonina was made squadron commander, so now I get to tease her and call her Junior Lieutenant Palova and she gets to boss me around. She doesn't though, not really. I think she's very proud of herself, but she doesn't act all big-headed and full of herself. Although, if she did, we'd bring her back to Earth pretty quickly, since we're all so down to Earth and honest ourselves. In fact, Sophia told her she wouldn't listen to Antonina if she got too bossy, even though we all know she'd have to.

Oh, another thing Evdokiia is having us do is extra training. I'm training Valentina to navigate and I'm sharing the flying with Antonina. She flies to the target and I fly home. Sometimes it's the other way around. After the first time out for the night, she sleeps a little when I fly and I sleep when she flies. We're only sleeping for two to four hours during the day, so every little bit, even a few minutes in the cockpit, helps. I'm sure you're getting about the same sleep as I am. Sometimes I feel so exhausted, but we go on singing and laughing to keep ourselves going.

A funny thing happened the other day. We got a visit from another regimental leader, who was curious about the girl's regiment. Evidentially, we're quite the curiosity around here. Sometimes I think they'd forgotten there's a war on, because they stop and stare so much. Anyway, we'd just landed for the morning and took off our flying helmets. The major stared at us and shook his head and pointed at Antonina.

"What a shame you decided to cut your hair so short, that's what a real girl should look like." He didn't understand why we all laughed so hard, but we hated cutting our hair in the first place. I can't wait to have my plaits back, although short is much easier to keep clean.

Anyway, I've rambled on enough and probably bored you to tears. I got your letter, in case you were wondering. Please write again if you can, I liked getting it. Stay safe and keep working toward our victory, so I can see you again.

Sincerely, Nadia.

I lay the pen on the grass and screwed the lid back on the bottle of blue ink. I blew across the paper to dry it and then reread my letter. Should I have called him Kolya instead? Nikolai seemed so much less personal, but Kolya was so familiar. I chewed my lip and considered crossing out Nikolai and changing it. Maybe I shouldn't write any of it. I could get into big trouble for sharing such information. It felt good though, having written down my thoughts, even if I had to rewrite my letter and burn this one.

My hand hovered over the pen, lying on the dirt beside me. Before I could make up my mind, I heard a ruckus coming from across the field.

Peeking out from under the Po-2's lower wing, I watched as an excited crowd started gathering near the airstrip. Men and women were crowded around a recently arrived aircraft. A large one for transporting people. I'd vaguely heard it land, because its engine was unusually loud, but I hadn't paid it much attention. Planes came and went all day, so one more was usually of little consequence.

"What's going on?" I called up to Valentina, who had been repairing holes in the wing on the opposite side of our machine. Where the other girls were right now, I wasn't sure.

"I have no idea," she called back. "Should we go and find out?"

I considered her question. We were flying to our auxiliary field soon and I needed to double-check my maps. Every new field made me a little scared I'd get us lost on the way there. I had heard about another regiment that had lost two aircraft in dense cloud cover, which had come over them suddenly.

One pilot had managed to reorient themselves and set down just in time, but the bodies of the other pilot and their navigator had washed up on a beach days later, having been lost too far out to sea to return before they'd run out of fuel. Such stories made my blood run cold and I was determined not to let it happen to us. Dying in battle would be bad enough; dying by my own error was unthinkable.

I shuddered and chewed my lip. On the other hand, it might be nice to stare at something and not be the one being stared at, for a change.

"Yes, let's go," I answered finally. I hastily folded my letter, grabbed up the ink and pen and rolled sideways out from under the wing. I'd learnt long ago that it was the easiest way to get out without bumping my head. Of course my friends pointed out if I didn't sit or lie under the wing, then I wouldn't risk hurting myself at all, but I found it a comforting to place to be. It felt private, but gave me a great vantage point from which to see the whole field.

I tucked my letter into a pocket in my uniform shirt and left the ink and pen beside my maps. Hopefully they'd be safe enough there. They'd be difficult to replace this close to the front. The letter, I trusted to no one but myself until it was sent, not even my friends.

I hurried after Valentina, not at all surprised to see Antonina, Sophia and the rest of my regiment already gathered, watching the spectacle. I tapped Sophia on the shoulder and she moved aside a little to let me in.

"What's going on?" I asked, standing on my toes to look over the heads in front of me. Not that I was short, but some of the other girls were taller, and there were men in the crowd.

"German prisoner," she whispered excitedly. "A flying ace, apparently. He was shot down and captured by our people. He's being transported to a prisoner of war camp." I had no sympathy at all for the fate of one of our enemy, until I saw him. He had dried blood down one side of his face, from a wound in his temple. I didn't think the wound would be a fatal one. He had one black eye and bruising around the other. He wore a dirty, torn German uniform, the front of which was caked with mud or blood. He had short blonde hair and deep blue eyes, which he kept lowered, I assumed, in humiliation. Even so, I was shocked to see how young he was. Younger than me. Younger even than the babies of my regiment. He couldn't have been more than fifteen or sixteen.

The enemy were sending children to war, and we were sending him to a prisoner of war camp, in which he would probably die. I swallowed hard. I'd never seen a German up close before. From the air, it was easy to forget they were people as well. For a moment, I was actually sympathetic. I almost wanted to tell his captors to let him go, return him to his mama.

And then he raised his eyes. They were so cold and full of hate. They fixed on me and then swept left and right, taking in my regiment. His lip curled and he spat on the ground.

"Nachthexen," he said derisively. "Ihr dreckigen Miststücke!"

I didn't understand German, but I knew when I'd been insulted. It was peculiar how words could offend, even when I didn't understand their meaning. The intent was perfectly clear.

My eyes narrowed, but opened wide again in surprise when Valentina burst out laughing.

I turned my face and stared at her. So did the prisoner, he looked at her as though she were something he'd scraped off the bottom of his boot. Considering the state of his boots, that was particularly unflattering.

"He called us Night Witches," Valentina explained. "I think Night Beauties would be more appropriate, but oh well." She shrugged, but her eyes shone with humour.

"Why did he say that?" I asked, frowning at her, and at him.

She spoke to him in rapid German, to which, to my surprise, he actually responded.

"Because our planes sound like broomsticks passing overhead," she translated. "He also said there's a special reward for anyone who shoots one of us down."

My eyebrows rose. The German army was that scared of us girls. I somewhat liked the sound of the nickname: Night Witches. It suited us, and justified the faith people like Marina Raskova had in us. We'd made an impact on this war.

I couldn't help but smile at the prisoner, who returned it with a scowl. Antonina gave him a finger wave and we all laughed as he was taken to a waiting truck. He might die, but he'd managed to give us all a renewed purpose. I'm quite sure that hadn't been his plan, but that had been the outcome.

I linked arms with the rest of my crew and we started back toward our aircraft, laughing and singing "Night Witches, Night Witches," over and over again.

CHAPTER 18

"What *is* that?" I asked, peering down into the darkness. The last couple of months had been the worst of the entire war. We'd been pushed back, out of the Ukraine, and back into the Caucasus. The region had a long and bloody history of invasion, defeat and conquest, and here we were again, fighting to hold it. And fighting to push back into the territory we'd lost.

If the rapid rate at which we were moving airfields was any indication, we weren't being very successful. A field we used one night was overrun by the enemy the next. This made choosing auxiliary airfields particularly dangerous. On more than one occasion, the officer in charge of this duty would land, only to have locals run out of nearby homes and warn them to leave, the Germans had already arrived, or were about to.

The faces around me seemed to be getting more and more exhausted, tense and sometimes even despondent as the days passed. We sung more often, but the songs were darker and the voices a little more strained. We tried singing happy songs and dancing, but they inevitably gave way to solemnity.

"It's... No, it can't be..." Antonina's voice sounded high and disbelieving through the Po-2's intercom, as if she were trying very hard not to cry.

"Oh, it is. Those..." The pilot never swore, but I think she came close to doing it tonight. She cut herself just short. "They're burning our wheat."

With a sinking heart, I realised she was right. Our people had been so busy fighting or fleeing, that what I was seeing far below us was field upon precious field of flaming wheat. It was dry and burnt like paper, plant after plant going up, embers jumping across the stalks and grains to feed hungrily on our food supply. As it was, we'd been struggling to feed the people. The reports, which filtered through day after day painted a story that was increasingly bleak. The war was taking a heavy toll on us all and there seemed little we could do but wait for winter and hope to freeze the enemy out. And hope even harder not to freeze to death or starve ourselves.

At least the blazing wheat made it easier to find the Germans. It was like a beacon for kilometres. At this low altitude, I could almost make out individual figures moving against the light of the flames.

Our target should be right up ahead," I called through the intercom. "Just past the burning wheat. You'd think they'd harvest it though, wouldn't you?" Or force someone, most likely our people, to do it for them. Food had to be as hard for them to get as it was for us. Burning food, with winter so close, was a death sentence for many people. Too many people. At least the wheat gave us a landmark to navigate by.

"They were probably ordered to burn it," Antonina replied logically, evidently having regained her stoic composure. "I'm not sure their precious Führer cares whether they starve or not, as long as we do and they go on fighting. I've heard if they don't fight, they get shot, so either way…"

Either way, they'd die. Still, I'd prefer to go with a full belly than starve slowly, or freeze to death in the snow. The more I thought about it — and I was thinking about death a lot lately — there were endless truly horrible ways to die. When I went, I wanted it to be quick and preferably painless. And many, many years from now, after we'd won the war. After nights like this disappeared so far into our memories that they seemed little more than bad dreams.

"We're approaching the target now," Antonina's voice broke through my morbid thoughts.

I flicked my torch on quickly to check our bearing and the wind-speed. "A little to the west," I called out. I felt the aircraft shift as she corrected our heading.

"Can you show me where to aim please?" She turned the engine to idle, so all I could hear was the sound of wind in my ears. I was always surprised at how loud something was that I couldn't actually see.

"Happily, Senior Lieutenant," I replied, forcing some of my good humour to reassert itself.

I heard her make a rude noise though the intercom, and grinned. I hefted the flare over the side and pulled my arm back just before a tracer shell shot past the plane. Another half a second and I would have lost the whole appendage.

"Oh my," I muttered, holding my arm protectively with the opposite hand. "I think they know we're here."

"They're always on the lookout for us Night Witches," I heard Antonina cackle gleefully. She banked the plane in an easterly direction and our altitude dropped significantly as we came back around over the target. The slowly dropping flare illuminated the landscape below us.

I heard a click as Antonina pressed the release and dropped our bombs. She threw the aircraft into a nimble sideslip and took us quickly out of the line of fire. Her manoeuvre saved our lives.

Tracers burst upward, into the night, right into the piece of sky we'd just vacated. The fire was so rapid and concentrated I had no doubt we'd have been hit hard had she not moved so quickly. I could hear my own breathing, ragged from the sudden fright.

Searchlights lit up the sky, but they were looking where we had been. Antonina had restarted the engine and nimbly avoided them every time they moved.

"This is too close," she declared, sounding breathless herself. Another couple of minutes and we'd be safely away. I swallowed hard and tried to force my heart to slow. I didn't want to come that close again.

A second later, one of our bombs exploded, earlier than it should have. We used bombs with delayed fuses, deliberately set to go off once we were safely clear. We flew so low we could easily have been caught in the blast from our own bomb and blown out of the sky.

As it was, the shockwaves from the explosion rocked the Po-2, making it shudder violently. Pieces of shrapnel flew up at us from below, tearing several small holes in the wings and a large one in the cockpit floor beside my feet.

I felt a searing pain in my arm and leg and realised I'd been hit. A sudden burst of wet heat at the back of my left leg told me I was bleeding. I tugged off one of my gloves and reached down to feel a shard of metal sticking out of the underside of my calf. Although it hurt like nothing I'd ever experienced, I didn't dare to pull it out in case I bled even more.

"Are you all right back there?" Antonina asked, so at least I knew she was alive.

"Yes," I lied. "You?"

"I'm fine, but Valentina is going to be busy."

That was true. The Po-2 could fly as normal, but the poor thing was going to need some patching up, as was I.

I clenched my teeth the entire way back to the auxiliary field to keep from crying out, or just crying. I could feel the blood pooling up around my fingers. My head was starting to spin. I was feeling a little faint, but there was no point in me telling Antonina. It would only distract her and we couldn't get back any more quickly. I could only hope she wouldn't notice I didn't ask to take the controls.

The next fifteen minutes felt longer than the nine days I'd spent on the train going to Engels, or the months I'd spent waiting to find a way to the front. I closed my eyes and focused on trying to keep my breathing calm and even. I wanted to sleep, but I had to force myself not to. I had to stay awake, focused and alert. I ran through each letter in Morse code in my head, over and over. I thought about Nikolai and whether or not he'd received my letter. I thought about writing to him again. I thought about his eyes and kind voice. I thought about my parents and why I still hadn't heard from my mother. I sang my favourite songs to myself inside my head.

Anything I could think of, I did it, until I finally felt the wheels of the aircraft hit grass and roll. Every stone, every hole, every movement jolted the piece of shrapnel and made my eyes water. I hissed in pain and hoped Antonina couldn't hear me.

When the plane stopped, I forced out a breath, grabbed hold of the side of the cockpit and tried to stand. My leg couldn't support me and I collapsed back into my chair, breathing heavily, my head swimming.

"You're a terrible liar," Antonina's worried face looked over at me. She looked out to people I couldn't see and shouted, "Nadia needs help!" I heard the sound of running feet and vague words of concern from female voices.

Then I passed out.

*****

When I awoke, it was morning. I was lying under a blanket beneath a tree to the far side of the field. My leg was stiff, but no longer hurt, for which I was extremely grateful. My clothes must have been a frightful mess. Fortunately, I'd never heard of anyone being arrested for a uniform violation relating to bleeding on one's uniform. Not yet anyway.

"Morning sleepy head." I opened my eyes to see Antonina watching me from the base of another tree. "If you ever scare me like that again, I'll...I'll..." She shook her fist at me and grinned. "I'm glad to see you're all right." She looked exhausted and dishevelled herself. I suspected she'd been sitting there all night, watching me. It's what I would have done for her. We were sisters through all things, good and bad.

I smiled weakly and sat up on my hands. I had a bandage around my leg, between my ankle and my knee, but it didn't hurt more than a slight sting. I might have a scar, but no permanent injury that would send me to the rear. Not that they could have sent me without a great deal of protest.

"I'm so sorry." I saw our Po-2 parked forlornly nearby, its underbelly already patched. The girls must have worked quickly, while I slept.

"Don't worry about it," Antonina waved her hand dismissively. "We were done for the night anyway. Valentina and Sophia have been working on her all night. They've gone to get us some food. To be honest," she went on breezily, "Valentina is thrilled, because there is no way Evdokiia is letting you fly tomorrow, so she's going to get to navigate."

"I'm glad someone is happy," I said dryly. Inside, I wanted to wither. I'd let everyone down and now my crew was going to fly without me. Sitting back and waiting for them was going to be torture of almost the worst kind I could imagine.

"Oh she is," Antonina replied, pretending not to notice my ire. "And Evdokiia is too, because she's the first replacement we'll be using, so it's a test for us all. Actually, Sophia will be acting as mechanic, so don't hurry up and heal, they'll need all the practice they can get."

I lay back down and looked up at the leaves twisting and spinning in the autumn breeze. I fully intended to heal sooner rather than later, no matter how much practice other people might need.

CHAPTER 19

Watching my crew leave without me that night was one of the most difficult things I had ever done. It was harder than going up there with them and risking being killed. At least then, I was busy and useful. I wanted to travel to the auxiliary field with them, but I wasn't allowed. Perhaps I should have been glad of the rest, but I couldn't even sit in our newest form of accommodation, the dugout, without fidgeting. It was worse than being back outside Moscow, digging ditches and being told war was men's work. It was my work and I wasn't allowed to do it. I even asked to help when they got home in the morning, but to no avail.

"Please," I begged Sophia. "Let me hand you tools, the fuel can, something."

"Nadia!" She rounded on me and I backed up a step. I suppose I had been a little pushy, but this was important to me. I didn't volunteer to be an observer.

Sophia exhaled, her shoulders dropped and she gave me an apologetic look. "I'm sorry. But really, you get a night off from the war and you won't even rest? If it were me, I'd be curled up in my bed by now."

"No you wouldn't, "I replied. "You'd be climbing over everyone to help out. And you wouldn't take no for an answer either."

"Fine, I wouldn't," she conceded. "But you're not helping me. Senior Lieutenant Bershankskaia ordered you to rest, so you'll rest." I knew she was serious or she wouldn't be throwing Evdokiia's rank around like that. I waited for her to point out that Antonina had said the same thing, and she also outranked me, but mercifully she didn't.

"Fine," I scowled at her and hobbled off to a spot under a tree. I wrapped a blanket around myself and leaned against the trunk. Just because I couldn't help didn't mean I couldn't watch.

I shivered as the afternoon air became more and more frigid. One after another, the aircraft disappeared into the sunset until I was left alone in the last rays of the sun. Only then did I go into our dugout and curl up, trying to keep warm.

About half an hour before dawn I woke from a daze and walked outside, a dense fog settled over the field, making even the faintest of lights and flares flicker and dance like tiny ghosts.

I rose from my spot and wandered over to the command area. My stiff leg and cold body made walking slower, but I was determined not to show any discomfort. I wanted to fly tonight and I didn't want anyone thinking I was weak.

"No one else is to leave for a while," I heard Major Popov say as I got closer. "This fog is too thick."

Our base were now located in such mountainous terrain that fog was becoming a common occurrence. It made flying difficult, but landing was incredibly hazardous. The fact that the mountains served as a landmark to aide navigation was little comfort much of the time. Tossing down flares lit up the fog, the light bouncing off the low cloud and often not showing the land around it. Even taxiing along the ground wasn't without its risks, since pilots still needed visibility to avoid hitting people and other planes.

"How many more are still out there?" a senior lieutenant asked, peering into the fog.

"Several regiments," Popov answered. He glanced over to where I stood and scowled. "Including the women's." The sound of concern in his tone surprised me. I know we'd acquitted ourselves well, but this was the closest to an acknowledgement I'd heard from our division commander.

"Right." The senior lieutenant gave me a sympathetic look and reached to pat my arm. "They'll be fine."

We both looked over to the landing strip as we heard the thrum of an engine. The pop-pop told me it was one of our Po-2s.

A flare lit up the night and floated to Earth on its tiny parachute, a light dancing eerily from it. I shook my head slowly as I watched its slow, unerring descent. I was certain the muted light would do little to show the pilot where to land. All they would see from the air at even a lower altitude would be a glow; a halo of light in the fog.

Gradually, the engine became louder, the sound bouncing off the clouds and echoing so it became difficult to determine from which direction the aircraft came. The air seemed to vibrate; the Po-2 must be mere handspans from the ground. I peered through the dark, trying to make it out amongst the shadows. Before I saw it, I heard the thud of tyres on the ground and a rush of movement, diagonal to the landing strip tore past.

"I think they guessed," Popov commented dryly.

I wanted to cry with relief. At least they'd landed safely.

I heard the shouts of several women as they climbed out of the cockpit to drag the plane clear. Even in the fog I recognised Sophia, her tall frame pressed against the wing, shoving hard to roll the wheels along the ground.

Thank goodness.

Amid the chatter, I heard the pop of another approaching engine. The sooner Antonina and Valentina and our plane were safely clear of the landing area, the better. My heart leapt and I started over to help. However, before I took more than two steps, I was halted by a light pressure on my arm.

"Stay out of the way," Popov ordered. I resisted the urge to sigh, and nodded. "Yes, sir."

I supposed I would only get underfoot out there. I just wanted to greet my crew and make sure they were safe before the next plane came in.

I didn't have to wait long. Antonina hurried over to me and tugged off her flight helmet and goggles. Her expression was grim, tears shining in the first rays of dawn.

"That was awful…" She spoke brokenly, devastated. I gaped at her, trying to grasp her meaning.

Sophia and Valentina came to stand beside her, each putting an arm around her.

"It was the fog. It came in so quickly no one could see." Sophia was unusually sombre. "Two planes collided near the auxiliary field. Mara, Alexia and Klavdia are all dead. Katya…Evdokiia is bringing her back." She gestured toward the landing strip where another of our regiment was coming in to land.

The Po-2 hit the runway with considerably more finesse than Antonina had and we all hurried forward to help Katya climb out.

The pilot looked dazed, her skin as pale as snow, a gash across the side of her head, but she was alive. With a sob of relief I walked over, embracing her briefly as the other women crowded around, trying to help her walk when her legs almost buckled under her.

"Mara," Antonina said softly, so Katya couldn't hear. "She was killed by a tracer shell before they even left the target."

My heart sank. Poor Katya flying alone through the fog, knowing her navigator was dead and just hoping to get herself and her sister's body back safely.

The bravery of these women was breathtaking and inspiring. I was in awe of their courage and devastated by their loss.

"We are going to be poorer for the loss of all three of them," I said softly, my voice reverent in this place of so much tragedy and death. "I'm thankful the three of you, and you two," I nodded to Antonina and Valentina, "got back safely."

If we didn't have each other, and our unbreakable bond, we would have wilted under the strain of all the loss. Nothing would make this life easier, but our friendship made it bearable, and the knowledge our division commander was starting to respect us did buoy me, even in the face of heartbreak.

I grimaced at Antonina as we started back to the auxiliary field to pack up so we could all get to bed.

"By the way," I said. "What was that exactly? I don't think I've ever seen anyone land diagonally before. Are you trying out a new technique?" I smiled faintly to show I was teasing and got a sock on my arm for my trouble. Levity amongst comrades was little more than a coping mechanism, but it was an affective one.

"I was trying to land!" she replied.

"Oh, because you know Major Popov was watching and you're probably going to get arrested for landing like that."

She groaned. "But I landed the plane and no one got run over."

CHAPTER 20

"Tell us again about Baba Yaga," I begged.

For much of January, the skies had been too dangerous for us to fly. Snowstorms had hit too often, leaving the airstrips covered in a layer snow and ice. The aircraft often had to be dug out of banks of snow, which sometimes reached their upper wings. Engine parts froze and had to be thawed or replaced; if the plane was on the ground, that was. Having the engine freeze up while the plane was in the air was almost certainly a death sentence. If being forced to make an emergency landing didn't kill the pilot, and anyone else on board, then the cold most likely would.

As often as not, we'd be ready to fly, we'd be given our orders and had the target marked on maps, only to have missions cancelled at the last minute. When we'd already traveled to our auxiliary field, this was particularly awful. Waiting on a cold field in winter was miserable, no matter how many layers of clothing we wore. The thought of the enemy freezing to death in inadequate uniforms cheered us somewhat, although we acknowledged the morbidity of our glee. Better they die than us.

Tonight, our mission had been cancelled hours in advance, which we always much preferred to the last minute change in plans. It gave us time to rest and have a rare moment of actual relaxation. So rare during the war, we made the most of these nights. We rugged up in gloves, scarves and blankets and huddled in our tiny dugout, most of the regiment pressed together for warmth. It was a tight fit, but no one minded.

We listened to the bitter wind whistle past; grateful we weren't out in it, but in good company with our wonderful sisters.

Antonina had six younger brothers and sisters and had had to look after them while her parents worked. She'd spent many, many nights telling them folk stories to help them get to sleep. Because of this, she was the best storyteller among us, or at least the only one who would admit to the skill, so we'd nag and pester her like little children to tell us some of her tales on those long, cold nights. She'd always sigh as if put out by the request, but then she'd clear her throat, settle into a chair while we lay on the floor and start talking. We'd all listen rapturously.

"Once upon a time there was a man who lived alone in a hut with only his young daughter for company. His wife had died many years ago, but they were very happy, just the two of them, together. They used to smile at each other over an old wooden table which they'd piled with bread and jam."

I licked my lips at the thought of both.

"But then, one day the man decided to marry again."

"Silly man," Sophia commented. "Mind you, who just decides to get married and a woman just turns up?"

"Shhh," I said, laughing.

"Yes, " Antonina went on, smiling. "The man became very silly in his old age; he was about forty after all. And he married, and the poor little girl had a wicked, terrible stepmother."

"Why are stepmothers always horrible in these stories?" Valentina asked. "I'm sure there are plenty of nice ones."

Antonina ignored her. "After that, everything changed. There was no more bread and jam on the table. Only stew made from funny, gnarled roots of old trees. But worse than that, the girl was not allowed to sit at the table at all.

"The stepmother said everything that went wrong in their cottage was fault of the girl. If the stew got burnt, it was because the girl had put too much wood on the fire. If it bubbled over, it was because she'd turned her back.

"And the silly, silly man believed his new wife, because she'd put a spell on him. He said no more kind words to his little daughter, which made her very sad. Deep down, he knew he was doing wrong, he just couldn't make himself stop.

"Day after day, the stepmother would say the little girl was too naughty to sit at the table with them. That she'd done this wrong or that wrong. None of it was true, of course, but the girl didn't dare to talk back. Then the stepmother would throw the girl a crust and tell her to go away and eat it somewhere else.

"The poor little girl used to go away, all by herself, into the old shed in the yard, which was little more than an old lean-to. She would wet the dry crust with her tears, and eat it all alone."

"That's disgusting." I wrinkled my nose. Salty bread didn't sound at all appetising. I think I'd have preferred to eat it dry.

"Shhhh," Sophia and Valentina said at the same time. I stuck my tongue out at them both.

"The girl often cried for the days before her silly father had remarried, especially for the days when her beautiful mother had been alive. But mostly she cried because she was all alone, and her loneliness made her sad.

"One day she met a little friend in the shed. He was a tiny, thin grey mouse who lived in a hole. He came out of his hole, with his tiny pointed grey nose, long white whiskers, little round grey ears and round black eyes, and his long, long pink tail. He sat up on his back legs and looked at the little girl.

"The girl took a corner of her crust and tossed it to the mouse, hoping not to scare him away. She knew how timid mice could be, but he looked lonely, just like her. The mouse gobbled the bread in one bite. She gave him more and he ate it too. And another bit until all of the crust was gone and she had none for herself. She didn't mind, because she was happy seeing him happy.

"The mouse looked up at her and squeaked, 'Thank you.' Then he added, 'Your stepmother is the sister of Baba Yaga, the witch.'"

"Is she a Night Witch?" Valentina asked. We all laughed. It took a while for Antonina to compose herself well enough to go on.

"If she ever sends you to take a message to her sister, come and tell me, because Baba Yaga would eat you with her iron teeth if you did not know what to do."

"Can she eat Nazis?" Sophia muttered.

"'Thank you,' said the girl, although the mouse's tale sounded a little odd. Just then, she heard her stepmother calling her to come in and tidy the house.

"The next morning, when her father went out, her stepmother called to the girl, 'I want you to go and see my sister. You will ask to borrow a needle and some thread.'

'But you have them in your sewing basket,' said the girl.

'Do as you're told,' the stepmother snapped angrily. 'Follow the road into the forest until you reach a fallen tree. You turn left and follow your nose and you'll find her easily enough.'

"The girl wanted to go into the shed to talk to the mouse, but her stepmother was watching her, so she didn't, she went straight down the road. When she reached the fallen tree, she turned left."

"How did she know it was the right tree?" Katya asked, lying on the other side of Valentina.

"Because she just does," Antonina replied. "Anyway, suddenly the mouse jumped out onto the road in front of her.

'Oh mouse,' she said, whatever do I do?'

'Easy,' he replied. 'Take the things you find on the road and they will help you.'

"The girl kept walking and found some strange things lying on the road. She found a new handkerchief."

"I hope it was clean," I commented.

"I doubt it, Valentina replied, smiling wickedly. "It was lying on the road."

"Do you want me to go on or not?" Antonina asked.

"Yes."

"Well then, the girl picked it up and put it into her pocket. Then she found a bottle of oil and some scraps of meat. She picked them up as well. Then she found a ribbon and a loaf of fresh bread."

"Mm, fresh bread," said someone and we all sighed.

"And then she came to the hut of Baba Yaga, the witch. There was a high fence round it with tall iron gates. When the girl pushed them open, they squeaked as though in pain. The little girl felt sorry for them. She pulled out the bottle and oiled them.

"Baba Yaga's hut was built on hen's legs, which walked around the yard. In the yard was Baba Yaga's servant. She was crying because of the jobs Baba Yaga made her do. The girl handed her the clean handkerchief," Antonina gave me a cheeky smile.

"Near the hut was a thin dog, chewing on a meagre crust. The girl gave him the bread she'd found. The dog gratefully gobbled it up and wagged its tail.

"The girl walked up to the hut and knocked on the door.

'Come in,' called Baba Yaga.

"The girl opened the door and went inside, and there was Baba Yaga, the witch, weaving on a loom. In a corner of the hut was a thin cat.

'Hello aunt,' the little girl said.

'Hello, niece,' said Baba Yaga.

'My stepmother has sent me to ask you for a needle and thread,' the girl said, trembling.

'All right,' said Baba Yaga, smiling, her iron teeth showing.

"Oh, the girl's stepmother is so horrid." Katya shuddered. "Not at all like my stepmother. She's nice."

"Anyway, Baba Yaga agreed to get a needle and thread if the girl would sit and weave for her for a while. As she walked away, Baba Yaga told the servant to make the bath nice and hot and scrub the girl clean, because she would make a nice meal.

"The girl smiled at the servant and told her not to hurry with the water and to carry it in a sieve. The servant nodded, but didn't speak, because she was scared Baba Yaga would eat her."

"Probably," Sophia replied. "Although you'd think the stepmother would be fattening her up, not starving her on crusts."

"Maybe she likes bones?" I suggested. "The dog and cat were thin as well, remember? Maybe one of those was dessert?"

"Yuck Nadia," Valentina groaned. "All of this talk about food is making me hungry."

"You're always hungry," Katya teased.

"I am not," Valentina argued. "Well, all right, I am. But we all are."

I murmured my agreement and nestled down deeper in my blanket. "At least we're warm."

"You might be," a mechanic named Tanya groaned. "You're not lying next to the door. Do you want to swap?"

I picked up my head and looked at her, "Not really, no. But thanks for asking. At least you're not having to sit out there and listen for the radio." No one liked doing that on a night like this. I didn't envy the radio operators at all.

Tanya snorted.

Antonina gestured for quiet and went on.

"As the girl wove, she looked over to the thin cat. 'What are you doing cat?'

'I am waiting for a mouse,' the cat meowed. 'I'm so hungry.'

"The girl gave the cat the meat she'd found on the road."

"I hope the meat wasn't from the last child the witch ate," Sophia said, grimacing.

"Yuck!" we all exclaimed.

"Anyway, the girl wanted to run away and go home. 'I'll weave for you,' mewed the cat. 'Baba Yaga will hear the loom and think you're still here.' So the thin cat took the girl's place and started weaving.

"The girl snuck out the door, toward the gate. The dog saw her and started to growl. Then it stopped, remembering the bread she'd given him. He wagged his tail and followed her to the gate. The gate, remembering how she had oiled its hinges, opened for her.

"Just beyond the gate was a tree. It had skinny, gnarly branches that reached out for the girl, trying to grab her and hold her for Baba Yaga. She tied the branches up with the ribbon and ran all the way home."

"When she got home, her stepmother was gone and the girl and her father lived happily ever…"

Antonina stopped, mouth agape as the door of the dugout swung open. I was so involved in the story I actually squealed in fright. There, in the doorway, stood not Baba Yaga, but Evdokiia Bershankskaia, tears rolling down her face.

"Marina Raskova is dead."

CHAPTER 21

We sat in stunned silence for what felt like years. No one moved, I don't think anyone even breathed. Any sound, any change might mean we'd have to accept it as the truth, and not a nightmare brought on by listening to scary tales. I blinked, but I knew I was awake.

I don't know who moved first, but from one moment to the next, we were all on our feet and pulling our commanding officer into a huge embrace. Someone, Tatiana I think, closed the door, cutting off the blast of freezing air, which I hadn't noticed until it was gone. Strange that I hadn't, since it was making the tears which rolled down my cheeks even colder.

I found myself with Sophia's arm around my shoulder, both of us crying, too shocked for a long time to speak.

It was level-headed Antonina who finally led our regimental commander to a chair, sat her down and crouched in front of her, Evdokiia's hands in hers. She spoke softly, but somehow everyone heard and turned to listen.

"What happened?" Valentina pulled a handkerchief out of her pocket and handed it to Evdokiia. She wiped her eyes and sniffed several times before she gained enough composure to speak. I almost wished she wouldn't. I didn't want to hear or face the truth. Of course, people died in war, but not the indomitable Marina Raskova. She was supposed to somehow be immune from all this — invincible in the face of German guns. Invulnerable to fascist bombs, inviolable because every one of us would have stood between her and the entire German army and offered our lives to safeguard hers.

Evdokiia took a shuddering breath and spoke: "The 587th was on its way to Stalingrad." She swallowed, took another breath and gained enough composure to go on. "Two of their planes had engine trouble and had to stop at another airfield. Marina — she went back for them."

That didn't surprise me. She wouldn't have wanted to rest until she knew where everyone was. She wouldn't have wanted anyone left behind. It was also like her not to send someone else to find the aircraft. She had always had such a personal stake in every aspect of the three women's regiments. I doubt much had gone on, even when we were at the front and separated, that she hadn't known all about. Every base, every mission, every death, every detail.

"The planes were fixed," Evdokiia went on, her tone more even as if she'd decided to get through the telling as stoically as possible. "They were given a clear flight path from Moscow to Stalingrad." She paused for another deep breath. How she managed to speak without crying, I don't know, because I was barely hanging on myself. I wanted to listen, needed to hear, but sobs threatened to overpower me.

"They were wrong," Evdokiia said softly, so I knew she had apportioned blame for whatever had happened. "The weather was appalling. They couldn't see anything, including each other."

I glanced over to Katya, whose blue eyes were huge. She was obviously remembering exactly what that was like. As I watched, her skin paled and her lips started to tremble.

"Two of the aircraft made a forced landing, but Marina's...it crashed."

My eyes swung back to Evdokiia in complete shock. For a long time, my mind felt numb, unable to comprehend her words. Nowhere in any part of my mind had I even begun to imagine this was what she had been going to say. Not only did it defy my understanding, it defied my very belief. And I wasn't the only one.

"What?" Sophia asked, her expression like thunder, clearly rejecting what she'd just been told. "Did you just say her plane crashed? Because of the weather?"

"That's exactly what I'm saying."

If Sophia hadn't been half-leaning on me, I think she might have fallen, because her knees gave way. I helped her down to the ground and sat myself. And then I burst into tears.

My idol, my mentor, my mother figure, my friend, was dead. I covered my face with my hands and wept, unashamedly, my whole body shuddering with each sob. I felt Antonina and Valentina join Sophia and I on the floor, and somehow we were all in each other's arms, crying bitter tears. We cried for our friend, we cried for our sister regiment and we cried for the unfairness of it all.

Before they were due to leave for the front, the 587th had received a shipment of brand new PE-2s, state of the art, top of the line bombers. Because they were so new and difficult to fly, the entire regiment had had to stay at Engels to learn how to fly them. Then winter had hit. It wasn't until now they'd been assigned to the front. They'd been on their way to their first mission.

After all of her rallying and hard work to get us together, after all she'd done to train us, after preparing us for battle, Raskova had died before she even got to see combat herself. And that, to me, was the greatest unfairness of all. This had been her whole life for over a year and she'd been so close. And to die now, because of the weather.

My eyes hurt and my head ached by the time I managed to regain my composure. It wasn't through willpower I was able to regain it either, it was because of Lena Turova.

"What now?" she asked, trying to look as though she didn't care, although her wet, red eyes said otherwise. "What's to become of the 587th? And us?"

I hated that she thought of herself at this moment, but I had to concede she was right. Raskova had formed the women's regiments; she'd pushed for everything we had and everything we'd done. Without her, what were we? And who apart from us, would care about our existence?

"The 587th has no commander," Lena pointed out. "Will they be disbanded? Will we?" I saw her mind turning over and didn't like what I saw. There were other regiments, men's regiments. At best, we might be distributed to those. At worst, we'd be sent home, or to the rear, where we might be lucky to help patch up men's aircraft or dig ditches or tend wounds.

I glanced at Antonina and saw her thinking furiously as well. She looked troubled and I suspected she was coming to the same conclusions. Her eyes looked a little panicked, which was unknown, for her.

"No." Our commanding officer's firm tone broke through all of our thoughts and made our faces snap toward her instantly. I couldn't help the germ of hope that flared in my chest.

"The 587th has a temporary commander. They'll continue as planned until a permanent replacement is assigned them. We will be staying together. We have a valuable role to play and we'll continue to play it. We have already justified her faith in us and we will continue to make her proud."

Senior Lieutenant Bershankskaia's eyes swept around the entire dugout, looking at every, single, one of us, giving us strength as we remembered Raskova wasn't the only one who believed in us.

"We will persevere, we will persist and we will prevail," she said, paraphrasing

Raskova's speech to us. It seemed like a lifetime since she'd said those words. "We will win. In the meantime, we will mourn. Sleep while you can, tomorrow we'll hold a memorial service after breakfast. We will honour her memory by saying a few words, and then we will force the fascists back, out of our homeland."

I wanted to applaud, but I simply nodded instead. I doubted sleep would come, but I'd try.

*****

I was walking though a dark forest, so dark I could only make out the outline of the trees above my head. There was no moon and no stars to light the way, I put out my hands to help guide me, but every time my fingers grazed a tree trunk it was warm and writhed under my touch. I kept on jumping, startled by the sudden movement, which would stop as soon as I moved away.

I looked back the way I'd come, but saw nothing but blackness, as though the world had been swallowed behind me. I had no choice but to keep walking. I put my hands out in front of me and took another few steps. I touched another tree trunk, but this time my fingertips seemed to fuse to the wood. I felt as though my hands were being drawn in deeper, sucked in by the tree.

I tugged my hands back, but they wouldn't move. My knuckles, my palms, my wrists, bit by bit, I was becoming a part of the tree. I tried to scream, but no sound came out.

"Please," I begged the tree. "Please let me go."

"I can help you," a low voice said from behind me. It was a strange voice, like the rustling of leaves had somehow formed words. "I can help you, but you have to give me something in return."

I didn't think, I just screamed out, "Help me, help me!"

The voice cackled softly and my blood ran cold. I saw her moving around behind the tree, rubbing her bony hands together.

"You made a deal with Baba Yaga," she said gleefully. Her mouth opened, showing two neat rows of iron teeth, pointed like knives. She opened her mouth wide, wider, her jaw dislocating, as she opened her mouth so wide her eyes and chin were hidden. Her tongue flicked out, looking like an angry snake.

She lunged forward. I cried out, terrified she was going to eat me. With a snarl, she bit the tree in two and my hands fell free. I staggered back and fell onto my backside. Wincing with the pain, I inspected my hands. They seemed perfectly fine, as though they hadn't been stuck in a tree only moments earlier.

I counted all ten fingers and looked over my wrists. When I looked back up,

116

the tree was standing again. I rose to my feet and stared. There wasn't so much as a tooth mark anywhere on the trunk.

I shook my head. "What?"

"You asked for help from Baba Yaga. Baba Yaga gave you help."

I wondered if Baba Yaga always referred to herself in the third person.

"Now it's time for Baba Yaga to take what was offered," she cackled softly and resumed rubbing her bony hands.

I took a step back. "I didn't agree to anything," I argued.

"Of course you did," she said, stepping forward like a thin cat hunting a defenceless mouse. "You asked for Baba Yaga's help. Baba Yaga never helps unless there's a price. Now, your price, my pretty one..." She reached out to stroke a bony finger over my cheek, her long nail-like claw passing in front of my eyes.

"From you, Baba Yaga will accept your youth. It's been a long time since Baba Yaga was young and pretty. Baba Yaga can catch many more young men with your pretty face."

Her hand turned and she cupped my cheek, her nails digging right through the skin. A searing pain ripped though my entire body and I screamed.

"Nadia. Nadia, wake up." I felt someone shaking me and my eyes popped open. Sophia was looking over at me, a look of concern on her face. "You were having a bad dream. I thought you wouldn't wake up for a while there. You kept on screaming 'help me, help me.' Are you all right?"

I picked my head up looked around and saw the dugout, my regiment curled up safely inside, some snoring, others sleeping quietly. I lowered my head again and nodded. "Yes, it was just a bad dream." At least this one, I could wake from.

CHAPTER 22

I didn't sleep again for the rest of the night. I didn't even try. It wasn't that I was afraid of bad dreams, goodness knows I'd had enough of them over the last year. I just didn't want to see Baba Yaga laughing at me again, those huge, horrible iron teeth gnashing, terrible eyes coveting me and my smooth skin. I had loved tales like that as a child; my older brother would tell them to me late at night, when we were supposed to be sleeping. The thrill of being scared was much more compelling back then, and much less real.

I was never going to ask Antonina to tell that tale to us again either. Maybe, I reasoned, if we'd gotten to the part where the dog, cat and mouse help the little girl to escape, I wouldn't have dreamed about it at all. Or maybe it was simply the news of Raskova's death that played these subconscious tricks on my mind.

I sighed and rolled over, only to find Sophia's elbow in my back. I rolled back again tried to get comfortable without disturbing the resting women around me. I let my mind wander and by the time it was morning, I'd forgotten all about Baba Yaga and just wanted to get back to work. Instead, we gathered outside, on the airfield, in the icy breeze. We were dressed in coats, gloves and hats, but I doubted much would warm our hearts today. Even seeing the men's regiment turn out to join our memorial did little to lift anyone's spirits, although we all appreciated their support.

Tatiana Vetrova, one of the squadron commanders, stepped forward to speak first. The tall brunette always seemed so indefatigable, so it surprised me to see her looking so drawn and pale this morning. In spite of this, she it didn't show any outward sign of fatigue when she spoke.

"Major Raskova was our mother," she said, addressing all of us girls, her voice formal and respectful. Her eyes swept across us, taking in everyone, lingering on a few who looked particularly sad and sombre. We were dressed in our uniforms, looking as immaculate as we could with little opportunity to bathe or launder.

Those girls who had already been awarded a Hero of the Soviet Union medal wore theirs pinned to their chests. Raskova had one of those, I recalled. Today the girls who wore them seemed especially proud to share that with our idol.

"Even though she wasn't much older than most of us, and was the same age as a few of us," Tatiana acknowledged those who, like herself, were already in their thirties, with a curt nod, "Major Raskova was our guide, our mentor, the strut that held the wings of our biplanes in place."

Tatiana smirked and I visualised Major Raskova literally holding up the wing, but the image didn't even make me smile. She would have done it had she needed to and she never would have complained about the necessity. The absurd image deepened my grief, because I knew she would have laughed at it. But now she couldn't even do that. I chewed my lip to keep from losing control and sobbing.

"For many of us, for most of us, she was the reason we wanted to fly. She was the reason we volunteered to come and fight this war. One of them anyway. She was the reason we were allowed to. She insisted we, us young women, were just as capable, as men, and in some cases more so."

A murmur of assent rippled though the crowd, including from my own mouth. I glanced over at the men, who looked politely bemused. We were out-flying most of them, and they knew it, even if their male egos wouldn't allow them to admit it.

We flew more missions, bombed with more accuracy and were able to immediately replace any airwomen we'd lost. We rarely argued amongst ourselves as they did, and we never drank. Alcohol of any kind was strictly forbidden in our regiment, under threat of arrest. That was Bershankskaia's order, not the Air Force, who rationed ten millilitres of vodka per pilot, per mission. It was an order we were happy to follow, since we'd seen enough drunk men to know a regiment needed its people sober.

"We have proven every day our worth as airwomen, our dedication to our homeland; our ability to adapt, grow and fight. We have not crumbled under the pressure, we have not given way before the fascist tide, we have not run away to hide behind our mother's skirts. None of us are here because we were told to be here, we all came when Marina Raskova called. We came because we all had a duty to her. She is gone, her call is gone, but our duty remains. We will fight in her memory. We fight every day because she asked it of us, because our motherland demands it of us. We fight for her, for Raskova."

"For Raskova!" we all echoed. I wiped tears off my cheeks with my sleeve and realised I'd started crying again. It was different now, though. I was still grieving, of course, but Tatiana's words had changed something in me. She reminded me I didn't need to fall apart. I had sisters and a country that needed me. If I crumbled now, I would prove Major Raskova wrong. I would show her choice of me for this regiment was not wrong. She'd told me, so long ago, she and I were alike. This, above all things, I wanted to be true. I wanted her to be right. So I would be strong and show myself I could be as tough as she had been. I would be flexible enough to bend and not break.

I stood a little taller, my chin raised, back squared, hands folded in front of me. I would fight harder now, and never rest until the war was over.

*****

When all of the commanding officers had spoken, and all of the day's tears had been shed, we were dismissed. Before I could walk more than a few steps, one of the administrative staff handed me an envelope. I didn't even waste time thinking it might be from my brother, or about my parents, I recognised the handwriting immediately.

"Thank you," I smiled at the other woman and tore Nikolai's letter open. I didn't even mind that my friends gathered around to read over my shoulder.

My dearest Nadia,

My thanks for your last letter; it came at a time when I needed it the most. My regiment lost six men today, one of them was my closest friend. Do you remember Alexy from Engels? He was the one who was always teasing me for staring at you. He might have seemed childish and immature, and I suppose he was, but I assure you, he meant well. He knew how I felt about you, and kept pushing me to talk to you.

I want to berate myself now, for not having spoken to you sooner. I wish with all my heart that we'd had more time to talk and get to know each other better when we had the chance. I hope we will have that time, after the war. Sometimes I feel as though you're nothing but a beautiful dream, and this war is the only reality I have ever lived.

We have our victories. Don't think, dear Nadia, I spend all of my time wallowing about and wanting to go home. Yesterday, after our men were lost, we shot down the German aircraft that killed them. It was a great satisfaction to watch them crash and burn, incinerated by their own fuel. And yet, after these victories, I can never sleep. What I feel in the heat of battle is gone later, and I can't believe it was me flying the plane that killed these people. I have to think of them as not being people at all, otherwise I'd be consumed by all of the death. I'm sure they think about us that way. My commanding officer said they think of us as less than human; like animals to be herded, or a plague to be eradicated. I have to think like that, too. They look like a plague, from the air; like an insidious plague of rats that keep on coming, to kill us.

And yet, in those quiet moments, in the dark, I wonder if they're writing to girls, like I'm writing to you. Do they miss wives, children, parents? It makes me realise if I give in and think of them as less than human, I'll lose my humanity as well. And then, why fight at all? If we've lost that, then we, as a race, are lost.

Alexy would have called me a fool and told me that I think too much. He always said I should act more than I think, not the other way around. He said if he'd been me, he'd have talked to you the first time he'd seen you. He also said something I think you'd find obscene and maybe offensive, so I won't share that. He was crude, but he was a good friend.

His plane was shot down; I don't think I mentioned that. It crashed. I landed and tried to help him, but he was dead already. The Germans were shooting at me, my gunner and my aircraft. The Ilysha (what we called our Ilyushin IL-2s), was shot full of holes, but it still flew. We call it a flying tank, because it's so difficult to damage, lucky for me. Not so lucky for Alexy.

Anyway, I should go; I want to write to Alexy's mother with my condolences. I'm not sure what to say. Nothing will bring him back to any of us. I hope this war ends soon, so I can get back to you. Please stay safe,

All of my love, Kolya.

"I remember Alexy," Valentina sighed. "He was so handsome, but he claimed to be in love with a different girl each week. He said he was in love with me once, until I told him I wasn't going to let him kiss me, or do anything else. I said I didn't want a boy who would die in the war...." She sighed sadly, her eyes shining with tears.

"I wish I hadn't said that now," she added. "Although he did call me a tease."

I folded the letter and patted her arm. "You weren't to know what would happen," I said softly.

"I don't know," Antonina said thoughtfully. "He was reckless. On the other hand, they all were, except Nikolai. They were all so eager to go out there and kill and die. Such a waste...so many young men."

"And women," Sophia added. "I wish the weather would let up, I'm tired of you girls being grounded. It's dull and doesn't get Hitler out of the Soviet Union."

I muttered my agreement and put the letter in my pocket. I wish there was something I could do to make Nikolai feel better. I knew exactly what he was going through, and I knew there was little, if anything, anyone could say that would make it all right. He'd probably lose a lot more friends before the war was over. I also might.

"You're right," I told Sophia. "The sooner we get back up there, the better. I'm tired of waiting, tired of war and tired of the enemy. I want to get back up there. I want to fight. It's time the Night Witches flew again."

CHAPTER 23

We did fly again soon after. The weather cleared and everything started to thaw. It was still cool, especially at night, but nobody complained. We were just happy to be flying again. Every night up there was a night closer to victory, or so I hoped. I didn't voice that thought to anyone; no one spoke of victory as an 'if' but as a 'when', even on the worst days.

Our regiment had so many new recruits that some of the mechanics and armourers seemed to spend half of their precious time training them. They were all so young even those of us in our early twenties and with half a year of battle experience felt old beside them.

"What can I do next?" Oksana was all of seventeen, blonde, small and eager. She seemed to have a surplus of energy and was always following the other mechanics around; carrying their tools, watching them work, learning everything she could. Every time we'd land and her plane was still airborne, she'd be the first to hurry over and help, her and her friends Natasha and Unka.

"They're tiring me out, " Valentina said with a sigh, pulling her now shoulder-length hair into a ponytail and tying it back. "Did we have that much energy at Engels?"

I looked up from the map I was looking over and shrugged. "I think we did, early on. Now we're war-weary old veterans."

"But I'm only twenty!" Valentina exclaimed, half-feigned despair on her face. "And I've never been kissed."

Neither had I, unless I counted the one on my cheek from Kolya. I rubbed my forehead where a headache threatened. I felt about forty years old, or more. A lack of sleep for over a year took its toll more on some days than others. Marina Raskova had apparently had the ability to sleep anywhere and fall asleep quickly, but I didn't envy that. In the end, even that ability hadn't helped her.

"I wish we'd win this war so we can all get some sleep," I sighed. "I think I might sleep for a hundred years afterward." I looked up and saw the new recruits running alongside a taxiing plane. "We should tell them to conserve their energy, but I'd hate to be the one to put a dampener on their excitement." That would happen soon enough. At least they were eager to learn.

A few of the girls who had been unhappily poring over papers in administrative duties had started training as ground crew, which delighted them, although I knew some wanted to be flying. They might have lacked the energy of the young recruits, since they'd been working as hard and as or long as the rest of us, but they were just as enthusiastic. None wanted to be relegated back behind a desk.

Two days ago, we had changed to a new base, one out of the mountains this time, on the Taman Peninsular. The sea breezes, blowing off the Sea of Asov to the north, the Straight of Kerch to the west and the Black Sea to the south, were cold at this time of year, but it was more temperate than the mountains.

"It's too cold up there," Valentina shivered. Once, I might have made a teasing comment of some kind, but in truth she'd lost weight from rationing. We all had. I knew we ate better than a lot of other people, but we ate the same things, over and over and it became monotonous to the point where I almost dreaded eating.

"It's too cold everywhere, " Antonina replied. She clambered into the front cockpit and shifted forward, letting Valentina sit behind her. "It's a shame it's too cold to swim in the Black Sea. I've heard it's nice in summer, when not occupied by Germans."

"I thought Sergei would have been keeping you warm?" Sophia teased.

Antonina turned around and stuck out her tongue. Then she gave Sophia a cheeky grin. "Why not?" she asked. "He wants to marry me."

"They all do," Sophia replied. "You'll be lucky they don't start fighting each other in their jealousy. Oh Antonina, Antonina, run away with me behind the trees." She threw out her arms, mimicking a man chasing our friend around, begging for her affection.

"Oh get into the plane," Antonina said in mock exasperation, "or I'll leave you behind."

"And who will rearm your plane, Junior Lieutenant Palova?" Sophia replied, raising her eyebrows and grinning. That didn't stop her from hurrying into the cockpit and making room for me.

"I don't know," Antonina replied, calling over her shoulder. "Someone else would, I'm sure." I could see her grinning and hear Sophia laughing behind me.

I shook my head and got settled, my map bag beside me. These silly conversations and mock fights were the way we got through the night. That we could tease each other and never take it personally just showed how comfortable we were with each other. Since the death of Marina Raskova and Nikolai's last letter, I needed the banter more than ever. It would be too easy to push everyone away and keep them at a distance to avoid the risk of being devastated when they died. Instead, I chose to take comfort in my closest friends and have faith in our skills that we'd survive the war. Besides, none of them would have let me do that to them. We took care of each other, always.

Whenever we did lose one of our regiment, we'd cry on each other's shoulders and be glad we were be able to do so. The men, from what we'd seen of their regiments, had a different way of coping. Some would drink their rations and brood. Others would fight amongst themselves. Still others would get angry and swear vengeance, then not return because their anger made them reckless. In combat, a hot head would never prevail over a cool one. I preferred the support of my sisters over the grief and hatred. I think the men envied us, but they never copied us. I sympathised with them that their male pride would keep them from what came so naturally to us.

I glanced out of the cockpit, seeing the sun dipping toward the horizon. A few of the other aircraft had already taken off, heading for the auxiliary field. It looked to be a clear night, which was always particularly dangerous, especially two nights before a full moon. As lovely as it was, the moon could all too easily serve as another searchlight, surrendering our position, even as it made the targets below us easier to see. It was no one's friend. I doubted I'd ever think of the moon as benign again for as long as I lived.

The sound of an engine brought me out of my reverie. A Po-2 was heading toward our base. This happened occasionally, when our auxiliary field was being overrun by the enemy after having been chosen for us. It always made my heart sink, to think they were moving so fast they were seizing ground hours after it had been deemed safe. It was dangerous too, for the first crews who arrived at the fields, only to hurriedly evacuate.

"What the..."

The Po-2 was moving erratically, its wings dipping left, then right, almost falling into a roll before tiling back the other way. I squinted against the sunlight, trying to identify it.

"Isn't that Katya's...?" It was, although she had just left. The plane levelled out, but then lost altitude rapidly. My heart dropped with it. It was descending so quickly I don't know how it didn't slam into the ground. At the last moment, its nose rose and the Po-2 righted, but was still coming in fast.

"Oh no…" I stood up in the cockpit, ready to leap out if she needed help. Hadn't she been through enough, with the crash that killed three of our sisters? She'd been devastated. Anya's funeral was the hardest day Katya had seen out here. A few people had suggested she return home after that, but she'd refused. No one would have blamed her had she left, but I understood why she didn't. Her place was here, no matter what life, and death, threw at her. But now this…

The plane hit the landing strip and bounced like a ball, before skewing left, then right, almost hitting another plane before it veered off to the left again. It finally came to a halt, at the very edge of the field, its wheels half-hidden by tall, dry grass, just metres from a ditch.

I jumped out of our plane, my feet hitting the ground hard. Ignoring the discomfort, I started running, my heart pounding. I assumed the worst, that one or both of the women on board were injured, or worse. From all over the base, people came running, including a team of medics.

I stopped dead in my tracks as Katya and her navigator jumped out of their aircraft, screaming as though Baba Yaga herself was on their tails. They started running away from the plane, both heading in different directions. Assuming the plane was about to explode, I gestured for my friends to halt beside me. I couldn't see any sign the Po-2 was on fire. They burned so quickly it should have been obvious by now.

I could hear Katya yelling, but I frowned, trying to make out what she was saying.

"Mice! Mice!"

"What? Oh my!" Out of the cockpit of Katya's plane, several little grey mice leaped and raced off toward the grass at the edge of the base. They darted nimbly into the ditch and disappeared.

I stared in disbelief and then burst out laughing. The woman had survived a mid-air collision and was regularly shot at by the German army, but she was terrified of mice? She'd stopped running now and turned back around, her face pale, but a wan smile on her lips.

"What was that?" Valentina laughed. "Now we know why she doesn't like the Baba Yaga story with the mouse in it. It has a scary little mouse!" Everyone in earshot laughed, including Katya herself.

"I've always been afraid of them," she admitted. "But one ran over my leg and I thought it was going to bite me or run onto my face. I just panicked." At least now she was smiling at the absurdity of the situation.

"Let's make sure they're all gone," I suggested, walking toward the plane. The mice must have been chased out of the fields by the enemy burning our crops. "Maybe we should scoop up a few and throw them at the Germans." I doubted they'd run from mice, but it'd be fun to hope they would.

"Mouse grenade." Valentina giggled. "I'd rather throw a real one." I knew she'd been itching to go back up and navigate, but no one wanted to think about what might have to happen to have that come about, especially me. I had no intention of getting injured again to help my friend out.

"Good point. Although we have more than enough mice." The darned things had been in our food stores, our dugouts, our beds and our blankets. I thought I'd even seen one leap out of someone's boot this morning. Lucky she hadn't put her foot into it first. And now we'd have to check our planes for the horrid things. If I found any while we were in the air, I really would toss them over the side.

I climbed into Katya's cockpit and saw no more mice, but lots of droppings. The mechanics would have to clean that out later. In the meantime, the women would have to suffer the smell. It was probably no worse than the usual one of fuel and human sweat, but I was glad it wasn't my plane.

"You're safe," I told her cheerfully. "Lucky the mice showed their little faces now and not while you were over a target." We all shuddered at what might have happened. I jumped down from her cockpit and moved away so she could take off again. She was looking very sheepish, but I patted her back and stepped aside to let her climb back aboard.

CHAPTER 24

My Dearest Kolya,

I hope you don't mind me calling you Kolya. I was sorry to read about Alexy. I do remember him. My friends said he was very handsome and they're very sad for you. I'm glad you did talk to me and I don't mind that we only had a short time, because it was a nice time.

Anyway, I have some exciting news for you, although you may have already heard. The Germans have been retreating since January, when we retook Stavropol, Armavir and Maykop. Our troops landed in Novorossiysk in February. The Germans have been occupying the city since last September, but a group of fisherman have kept them from taking the port.

Anyway, our troops have been trying to force them out for weeks. Antonina and I, and the rest of my regiment (of course), have been bombing their positions in the city and outside so reinforcements can't reach them. We hope to beat them out any day now.

This week, four of my regiment went missing.

I put my pen down and rubbed my temples. The whole letter sounded a lot more upbeat than I felt. Even the thought that we had the Germans on the run and the war might be ending soon, did little to lift my spirits. The last week had been exhausting.

Once Katya and her navigator had taken off again, we'd followed. The auxiliary field was nothing special, although it did have a lovely view of the sun setting over the Kerch Straight. Not that we had time to stop and look. As soon as the light had surrendered to the darkness, our battle resumed.

We followed Lena and Inna Markova, with Katya a safe distance behind us. All of the others would follow, our usual three minutes apart. Our first sortie for the night went without major incident, apart from a few holes in the wings. It was nothing worth stopping to have patched up, so we refuelled, rearmed and took off again.

Katya's aircraft had sustained more damage and would have to stop for a while longer, surrounded by eager mechanics.

"Lucky her," Antonina had said dryly. She was very tolerant, but the line between the veterans and the new recruits was becoming all too clear. I hated the idea that our regiment had cliques, but until they'd been exhausted and bloodied, they wouldn't understand as we did.

"Who will be behind us now?"

I turned to squint through the darkness. "Alexa, I think, and Klavdia will be behind her." Alexa was a good pilot, and although she was also new to our regiment, she'd flown with a men's regiment before she'd transferred. She had a lot of interesting tales to tell us, but she admitted to finding us much easier to work with than the men had been. None of us ever tried to flirt with her or her touch her in places she didn't want to be touched.

"All right, ready for take off!"

Fifteen minutes later, we were back over the target. I wondered if I would ever stop being scared. Every time out was like our first. My heart raced, my palms sweated and I got wet under my arms. I could have almost held my breath the entire time, except I would eventually have passed out. Some nights, I thought that might be preferable.

Our second turn over our target, we were met with an eerie silence.

"This is odd," Antonina said through the intercom. She sounded concerned. "Nothing is firing at us."

I did think it a little odd. I looked down at the target, still lit by the flare, and saw no movement, no searchlights, nothing.

"Maybe we killed them all," I suggested, "Or perhaps they're surrendering."

"I'm sorry Nadia, but I don't believe it," Antonina said. Neither did I. The hair stood up on the back of my neck and I remembered what the German prisoner had said. They were giving extra rewards for anyone who shot down a Night Witch. They wouldn't give up this easily.

And yet, the target exploded right on cue and we soared away, heading back to our auxiliary field. Maybe I had been right. We might land and be told we didn't need to go back for the night, that the Germans were defeated. And then I saw sustained fire directly behind us. The Germans had been watching and timing us. They'd let us go, so they knew exactly when and where the next aircraft would come.

An anti-aircraft shell slammed into the right wing of Alexa's plane, all but tearing the strut in two. The wing sagged and in the searchlights, I watched the plane start to lose altitude. Alexa must have been steering like crazy, because the plane veered away from the target and headed in low, behind our lines and disappeared into the darkness.

Klavdia's plane was directly behind and I could hear as she too came under heavy fire. With my heart in my mouth, I looked over my shoulder, but all I could see were searchlights weaving back and forth though the darkness.

"The rest of the missions are cancelled for the night," Sophia told us as soon as our machine came to a full stop. "Evdokiia won't risk any more."

"Alexa didn't come back then?" Antonina asked.

I turned my face, keeping it in shadow so they couldn't see what I was thinking. Too many women had been shot down or had crashed. Alexa, Klavdia and their navigators were simply two more in what seemed like a continuous line of death.

"We need to head back to base," Sophia replied. "I'm going to ride in the truck." After only two missions each, there would be dozens of bombs left over. They would need to be returned to base before the Germans found our field and tried to take them. Sometimes the armourers would return to base with the truck, to help to protect it. I usually missed Sophia's company in the cockpit, but tonight I felt the need to have some time alone. She'd be better off too, not being infected by my bad mood.

*****

"No word yet." Senior Lieutenant Bershankskaia looked tired and drawn. "I've spoken to the radio operators. Everyone is keeping an eye out. They'll let us know when they hear something."

I frowned at her. "Don't you mean if?"

She looked at me in surprise, my curt tone very unusual for me. I didn't apologise though. I was tired of hearing 'when' and having 'when' never come. When the war ends, when we get better planes, when, when, when. Was I the only one who could see the hopelessness of our entire situation?

"Perhaps you should get some rest, Navigator Valinsky." Now I looked at her in surprise. I couldn't remember a time when she'd ever addressed me by rank or surname. I understood clearly though, she outranked me and she was pulling it. I had been rude though. I was lucky she didn't have me thrown in the guardhouse. Right now, I might not have minded. At least I'd have been alone.

"I'm sorry, ma'am," I said as deferentially as I could. "I didn't mean to…"

"Nadia." She put a hand on my arm and spoke more gently. "We're doing everything we can. We'll send out a search party in the morning. In the meantime, there is nothing more any of us can do but get some rest. All right?"

I nodded. "Yes, ma'am." I was chastised, but not appeased, not really. I hung my head and went to hide under my blanket in our dugout. When the rest of my crew came to rest and talk to me, I pretended to be asleep.

*****

I ate breakfast sparingly the next morning, glancing over at the places set out for Alexa, Klavdia and the two other women. This was something we had done since the first deaths, back at Engels. We set the place and left it set, even when we knew our sisters weren't returning. It was sentimental, on this I think we all agreed, but we acknowledged their lives and their contributions.

Today, it was a sign of hope. Hope I just didn't feel.

I sensed people looking at me, and knew my friends were concerned, but I kept my eyes lowered. For the first time since I'd met them, I didn't think there was anything they could say that would comfort me. I was exhausted in body, mind and soul. Somewhere in the back of my mind was the thought I was done. Maybe it was time to leave. I could go back to Moscow and look for my mother.

I didn't even know I was crying until I felt Sophia's arm around me, holding me and letting me cry on her shoulder. I don't know why I cried, only that it felt good to do it. How long I cried for, I wasn't sure, but my eyes hurt and my head ached by the time I'd run out of tears. My chest hurt from sobbing, but my heart felt strangely lighter.

"Thank you." I sat up and wiped my eyes with the handkerchief Valentina offered.

"It's clean," she giggled.

I couldn't help but smile, however wan it might have been. "Thank you," I said again. "Do you really think…" I glanced over the empty spaces and nodded my head.

"Anything is possible," Antonina replied firmly. "We just have to hope."

*****

I looked down at the letter I had started. I picked up my pen, dipped it in ink and went on writing.

It has been a long week, dear Kolya. We set a place for Klavdia, Alexa and their navigators for three days and three nights. Then a truck drove onto our base this morning. Klavdia and her navigator, Sonja, were sitting in the back. They'd been forced to land their damaged plane and then they'd had to walk for kilometres and kilometres before they found any of our people.

131

When they did, they came under attack. They spent three days in the trenches with the infantry, ducking bombs and drinking tea with the men.

It took three days to defeat the Germans and for a truck to be spared to return them to us. They were both happy we hadn't packed up their places at the table. It was good to see them sitting there again, as though they'd never left. They'll have to wait for a replacement plane though. It might be a few weeks until one arrives.

I'm sorry to say it's not all good news here though. The search parties found Alexa's plane. They had crashed into the sea, to the north of us. The plane was empty and their bags were gone. It seems they tried to swim to shore. Poor Alexa's body washed up on a beach the next day. Her navigator hasn't been found. We've had to pack up her place, because no one thinks she could have made the swim back to shore, it was just too far.

I long to hear word of more German retreats and the end of this war finally being in sight. My heart is heavy and I want to see you again, because thinking of you makes it lighter. I think a piece of my heart went with you when you went to the front and I need it to be whole again. I want to look into your eyes and see what I saw that day on the train.

Love, Nadia.

CHAPTER 25

After the death of Alexa and her navigator and the brief disappearance of Klavdia and Sonja, it was finally decided to put radios in our Po-2s. Had Alexa been able to radio for help, she might have been rescued. And of course, if Klavdia had been able to, we might have known they were alive much sooner.

"It's mostly so they can order us around when we're in the air," Antonina pointed out over her morning cup of tea. "Not for our safety."

"I thought it was so you could gossip with the other girls?" Sophia teased.

Antonina swatted her on the arm, grinning the whole time.

"She doesn't need a radio to gossip," I commented. "We do that anyway, through the intercom."

Antonina retorted, "We do not. One of us is usually asleep when we fly."

"That's true," I conceded. "After the war, I might need to get myself a bed shaped like a cockpit, so I can sleep."

"Just sleep in a chair," Valentina giggled. "With a footstool to rest your legs on."

I snorted. I was getting far too accustomed to sleeping sitting up. When I did lie down at night, I lay awake until I propped another pillow under my head.

"I'm not sure I can sleep without listening to Sophia snoring anyway."

"I do not snore!" she protested loudly. Everyone in the mess turned to look and chuckle. All of the girls had heard her; her snoring was legendary. Even some of the men had stuck their heads into our dugout to listen, and agreed that none of their regiment snored as loudly.

"Anyway," Antonina interrupted, "I heard the person who is going to be installing our radios is..." She paused for effect, her eyes wide. "A man!" She finished with a flourish.

"Oh no, not a man," Valentina giggled again, her eyes wide with mock horror.

Sophia, however, was frowning. "Can't one of us do it?"

"Evidently not," Antonina shrugged. "He's arriving this morning, after breakfast."

None of us could sleep after that, so we went out to the airfield, sat on the wing of our aircraft and waited.

Lieutenant Uri Nosal was the unhappiest looking person I had ever seen, and this was a war zone. He was handsome, in an odd sort of way, with a high brow and a nose like a falcon. His hair was dark brown and neat and his eyes were a startling blue. He had a strong chin and high cheekbones, making him look like a tsar or a prince. If not for his scowl, half of the girls would have adored him on sight.

He looked at us as though we were the most loathsome creatures he'd ever encountered. Commander Popov had been positively friendly compared to Nosal.

"I don't think he likes being assigned to a women's regiment," Antonina commented mercilessly, just out of his hearing.

"It's only temporary," I pointed out. "Maybe for a month?" If it took a full day to fit a radio to each plane, then he shouldn't need to be stuck with us for any longer than that.

"I bet he'll work faster than that," Sophia said, chuckling. "Hey Valentina, maybe you should offer to help him?"

Valentina opened and closed her mouth, then jumped up off the wing. "I will. I might just learn something, too. I've always wanted to know how to install radios." I thought she'd march off, but at the last second she grabbed my hand and tugged me off the wing.

"Come with me," she insisted. "I need moral support."

I followed along laughing. "No wonder the men say we always go around in at least pairs," I said. "We do." Even at Engels, no one had ever had to tell us not to go anywhere alone. We had always naturally fallen into pairs or groups and made sure to go everywhere together.

Not that the men around us had proven to be untrustworthy, but we still valued our safety and took no risks while on the ground. It might have been counterintuitive to fight the enemy army night after night and still be wary of our own people, but they were men and therefore unpredictable.

"He's handsome, isn't he?" Valentina sighed, watching Nosal closely while we approached. He was working on Tatiana's plane and had undone the first few buttons of his shirt. Technically, it was against regulations, but the day was warm. Many of the men's regiments removed their shirts entirely when the days were sunny and hot and no one ever told them off for it. I'm sure if us girls had complained, they would have had to wear them, but we never did. Most of the boys were good to look at, so we stared instead of protesting. I'm sure they'd have done the same, but of course we never walked around with our shirts off.

Valentina cleared her throat. "Excuse me, Lieutenant Nosal."

He looked over at us, his intense blue eyes catching the sunlight, just like the tropical ocean. I always had had a thing for men's eyes, of any colour. When I couldn't sleep at night and had trouble recalling specific features of Nikolai's face, I could always remember his eyes.

Nosal's eyes were almost enough to make any girl fall in love with him on the spot. I saw Valentina swallow. She must have been thinking the same thing.

"What do you want?" he snapped, making no attempt at all to hide his hostility toward us. He may have been nice to look at, but he wasn't nice at all. That didn't faze Valentina.

"My name is Valentina," she explained, her voice still friendly. "I'm a mechanic. I was wondering if you needed some help, because I'd really like to learn…"

"I need no help," he replied curtly and turned away.

"I'm sure you don't." She sounded a little perturbed, but not discouraged. "But I'd really like to learn, then when they stop working, I mean, if they stop working, I could fix them and you wouldn't have to come back and…"

He gave her such a cold look it cut her off mid-sentence.

"And I want to go back to my regiment. Sometimes in life we don't get what we want. I don't have time to teach women all of this technical stuff. You wouldn't understand it anyway. Now please leave me to work. I want to finish." He didn't need to add 'and get away from you girls'; the intent was obvious.

Valentina took a step back and I had to stop myself from taking a step forward. I had never wanted to hit anyone before, apart from German soldiers, in my entire life. Well, perhaps my brothers, but they were siblings. Hitting them came naturally. But this man, I wanted to wipe the look of supercilious superiority right off his handsome face. Maybe if I broke his nose, he wouldn't be so pretty.

Valentina must have seen my anger, because she grabbed my wrist and tugged me back to a safe distance.

"He's not worth it." She sounded so disappointed. It only fuelled my ire. "Don't get arrested for his sake. Save your anger for the Germans."

She was right, naturally. Punching Nosal would only have negative repercussions for me. Although he'd be a laughing stock for being hit by a woman.

"All right, all right," I conceded. "But he was so rude. If he'd been one of us, he'd have taught you every nut and bolt and wire until you could install radios in your sleep." Sharing knowledge could only help all of us and Valentina had a good point. If a radio broke, someone would have to fix it.

"I don't need to get to know his nuts anyway," she said crudely.

I shook my head at her, but laughed. Looking back, I saw Lieutenant Nosal watching us. Good, let him think we're laughing at him. His feelings were inconsequential compared to those of my friend.

*****

For a full week, all of the girls ignored Lieutenant Nosal, except for our commanding officers. I suspected they only spoke to him because they had to. Mostly, we were too busy to spare him any thought, apart from the hours he spent working on our Po-2. Antonina decided to tease him by leaving bunches of wildflowers around the cockpit. They smelled lovely, and very feminine.

By the time we were able to get back into our plane, several bunches had been squashed and the rest tossed off onto the dirt beside our aircraft.

"So we know what he thinks of flowers," Sophia grinned, looking over at where he sat, alone, in the mess hall. "Maybe you should have left something more manly."

"A live grenade?" Valentina suggested cheerfully.

"A nest of mice?" I said, grinning.

"Baba Yaga?" Antonina added.

We broke into laughter, although I shuddered, remembering the dream I'd had. I wouldn't wish the witch's iron teeth on anyone, even Lieutenant Uri Nosal.

I glared over at him, even though I knew he wouldn't look up at me. One of the administrative staff walked past, handing out letters and parcels and left one of the latter on the table in front of him. I recognised the packages we received occasionally which contained uniform requisitions.

I watched him open the top of the box. I had decided long ago that I could tell a lot from the way someone opened a box. The impatient ones, like Sophia, tore the cardboard, eager to see the contents. Patient people, such as Antonina, opened them carefully, leaving the flaps intact so they could be closed again and the box reused.

Nosal opened his with all the care of an engineer, as though the box would cease working if he wasn't careful with it. Men were so silly.

He opened the flaps and looked inside.

"What is this?" He might have tried to spend his time with us being as inconspicuous as possible, but everyone was looking at him now.

"What is this?" he demanded again. He shot to his feet, reached into the box and pulled out an item of underwear. For a moment I stared, watching his face turn a fascinating shade of pink, then red like my mother's borscht.

There, dangling from his fingers, was a small pair of white, women's underwear. They were the kind of knickers the Air Force had finally gotten for us, just before we left Engels. The kind we all wore because it was all we were sent when our uniforms were replaced.

"Is this some kind of joke?" He looked around at us and I couldn't contain myself any longer. I burst into gales of laughter. The rest of the women and most of the men in the mess hall started to howl as well. Nosal was not obviously a gendered family name, unlike Popov or Palova, so it might well have been an honest mistake. Still, it was hilarious.

For a while I thought Lieutenant Nosal was going to throw the box at someone and storm out of the mess hall. Honestly, I wouldn't really have blamed him, he must have been pretty humiliated. I think I would have run away and hidden for a few days. Or a few months.

He scrunched the knickers up in his hand and then, somehow, he must have seen the funny side of it. Gradually, his expression eased to a faint smile and then he began to laugh. He tossed the underwear at one of the men, who deftly caught it and threw it at one of his wingmates.

For a good few minutes, they got thrown back and forth around the mess before they finally ended up in Antonina's hands. She held them up in front of her, grinned and said, "Just my size," and tucked them into her pocket.

We all laughed, including Evdokiia, who I noticed watching closely from a corner table. Nosal transferred away a week later and a woman was sent to replace him in installing the radios. They never tried to send a man to our regiment again.

CHAPTER 26

"That wasn't so bad," Antonina commented, watching Klavdia's bombs explode over the target. "Only a few anti-aircraft guns tonight. I think the Germans are giving up on Novorossiysk. Or they're all dead." Either way, her voice through the intercom was cheerful and upbeat. I knew her well enough to know the slight reduction in resistance wouldn't make her complacent.

I was glad we'd been paired together. We made a great team and trusted each other with our lives. Had I been paired with Lena, I wasn't confident we'd both still be alive. The ability to communicate, both with and without words, was vital to our success and I would never have that bond with Lena. Only Inna Markova seemed to understand and tolerate her. Lena was still one of my sisters and I'd do anything for her, but sometimes we can't pick our relatives and she was one of those.

"Maybe if we aim right, they will all be dead," I replied. I had a few grenades I'd been handed before we left, and I was looking forward to tossing them over the side. The chance of hitting anything or anyone significant was probably slight. Still, I was happy to imagine my aim would be true enough to do some damage. If nothing else, it would annoy the Germans, and that was a good way to pass the time.

Antonina jokingly referred to it as our regimental sport, since we weren't really inflicting significant damage, just slowing them down a little.

"It'll never make the Olympics," Sophia had replied drolly.

"I should hope not," Antonina had said and laughed. "Killing people isn't really in the spirit of the Olympics."

I doubted flying in an ancient biplane, over enemy territory, under enemy fire, while dropping bombs and grenades on them were in the spirit of the Olympics either. How ironic that Adolph Hitler himself had attended the 1936 summer games and had been welcomed there. Seven years later, he was loathed the world over. Well after the war, he'd be dead and probably forgotten.

"You have good arm," Antonina said, reminding me where we were. The target was almost right beneath us.

I picked up a grenade and prepared to pull the pin.

"I'm sure you'll…"

Whatever Antonina had been about to say, she was cut off as we were suddenly caught in the junction between two searchlights. Anti-aircraft guns roared, shells flying past us like pieces of metal lightning. I ducked, pulled the pin out of the grenade and threw it over the side. If it inflicted any damage, I didn't have time to notice.

The nose of the Po-2 suddenly dipped and we were losing altitude rapidly. I pushed myself up a little higher on my hands and glanced around. I saw no fire, no damage to the engines.

"Antonina?" She must have been trying some new stunt; some way of dropping bombs lower than usual. We were often practicing and trying out new techniques, but it wasn't like her not to tell me if she was going to use one, especially one this drastic.

We were falling so fast I felt as though I was leaving my stomach behind. I trusted her so implicitly that for a few moments I hung on, before suspecting something was wrong.

I looked forward, into the front cockpit. Antonina was slumped over the controls, pushing them downward. It was her weight making the aircraft nosedive.

"Antonina?" I reached forward and shook her shoulder. When she didn't respond, I had no choice but to grab the back of her collar and tug her off the controls. With my other hand, I pulled on the controls in front of me, forcing the nose up.

I'd never been as glad to be in a Po-2 as I was just then. The sturdy little plane levelled as if nothing had ever happened and putted along, engine popping.

I banked the plane, sitting forward at an awkward angle, hanging on to the control stick with one, sweaty hand and headed away from the target.

"Antonina? Antonina!" I got no response from her at all. I was scared of choking her, but the moment I let go of her collar, she started to slump forward again. I had no way of holding her in place except with my hand.

"I'm so sorry," I breathed. I kept one hand on the controls, the other on her and kept looking out for landmarks as we flew. "Just hang on until we land," I said into my intercom. "Then we'll get you some help. Remember how you helped me when I was injured? You got the plane back without me having to navigate and that went fine. Remember? You didn't make a fuss of me, or get angry with me, you just got us home.

"Now it's my turn. I'll get us home and land and you'll get help." I prattled on and on, keeping up a steady stream of chatter. Even if she couldn't hear me, it was comforting to me.

"First sign of madness, they say. You'll laugh later, when I tell you I was talking to you like this. I don't care; you can laugh all you like, later. I could call ahead for help if I had a spare hand. They could light up the airstrip. No, I suppose they couldn't. That would only endanger other people. No, we'll be fine."

I took a few steadying breaths and searched for landmarks that would guide me toward the landing strip.

"Remind me when we land that we need to learn to fly and land with one hand," I said in a congenial tone. "Especially landing. I'm sorry if I bounce this."

I glanced over to locate the landing strip and gradually pushed the controls forward, bringing down our altitude. If anyone was in the way, I'd have to apologise to them later too, because this would be far from a perfect landing.

Somehow, I felt the wheels touch grass and let the plane glide along the ground, slowly, but gradually. We taxied around and came to a stop near the ground crews.

"I need help!" I called out, before the wheels had even stopped turning. I climbed over from my cockpit to the front one.

"Antonina?" She was looking back at me, staring with vacant, glassy eyes. A piece of shrapnel was lodged right in the middle of her forehead. Blood had trickled from the wound and soaked her uniform and the controls.

I think deep down I'd known she'd died the moment she stopped speaking.

*****

How I got back to my bed and under my blankets, I never knew. I think someone carried me; I was too deeply in shock to walk. I was given something to drink, which made me sleepy. I remember a cup being pressed to my lips. I'd tried to fight it, but they had insisted I drink.

I swallowed and tried not to spit it out. The taste had been horribly bitter. It burned all the way down. Somehow I didn't throw it back up. My eyelids felt heavy and everything else was a blur.

I woke tangled in blankets, my head pounding like a marching band.

"Tell them to go away," I muttered, sure there were drummers exacerbating

140

my discomfort.

"Nadia?" Valentina's worried voice made me wince.

"What did she say?" Sophia's voice asked from across the room.

"I don't know, something about wanting someone to go away."

A cool, damp cloth was pressed against my forehead. "Do you want us to go away, honey?" Valentina asked.

"No," I managed to croak. Then the memory of last night came flooding back. Had it been last night? I had no idea for how long I'd been asleep. It didn't matter. Antonina was dead.

"Bad dream?" I asked softly, hopeful. I cracked my eyes open.

There was a long heavy silence, during which I knew what her words would be. "No, I'm sorry. Antonina is gone," Valentina matched my volume, if not my tone. She'd have witnessed our landing. She had seen our friend. Her eyes were red. They were dry now, but she'd obviously been weeping.

"You got yourself and the plane back home," she said, sounding impressed and proud. It did nothing to make me feel better. It wouldn't bring our sister back. "Do you remember? You flew and landed with one hand. They're talking about giving you a medal."

"I don't need a medal," I muttered.

"No, I suppose you don't." I saw Sophia moved to sit down beside her. She'd been crying too.

"You were hysterical," she said. I could see the sympathy in her eyes; it hurt the worst of all. They'd lost a friend too; they shouldn't need to look after me. "You kept on begging Antonina to be alive, so they had to sedate you to bring you back to base. Katya flew you. She insisted."

Katya would understand better than anyone how I'd felt. I was glad she wasn't here now though, I didn't think I could bear to see sympathy in her eyes as well.

I struggled to sit up. I wasn't injured. I shouldn't be lying around like this. A glance toward the open door to the dugout told me it was daytime, most likely afternoon. I'd slept for more hours than I had throughout the entire year. Well almost.

"You should have woken me," I told them. I was angry with myself for using such an ungrateful tone.

"Not a chance," Sophia said. "Evdokiia would have had us both arrested if we had. She's been here a few times, everyone has. They were worried about you, about all of us."

All of us. *All of us* were no longer here. The ache in my heart was tenfold what it had been with all the other deaths. It sat like a weight, pressing me down, threatening to pull me in and drown me. I had no Baba Yaga to save me this time, no deal with a witch to give my youth in return for my friend or my sanity. I would have to hold it together.

"You're not alone," Valentina said gently. "You always try to be so strong for all of us. You're tougher than all of us, but I know you hurt inside too."

Her words floored me. I was tough? I didn't feel tough. I felt like a little girl, curled up under her bed because a boy at school had called her names and pulled her pigtails. I felt like the daughter who had cried because she'd let go of her mother's hand at the markets and gotten lost.

I wasn't tough, not at all. Not on the inside.

"There's something you should know," Sophia added, shifting awkwardly on the low stool she'd set herself down on. "I'm not sure I should tell you. Maybe Evdokiia was planning to…"

I frowned at her. "You have to tell me now." I drew a breath and steeled myself. I wasn't sure I could handle more grief, but better it come from Sophia than anyone else. "Sophia?"

She sighed. "Fine, you twisted my arm. You're," she paused. "You're going to be flying. Evdokiia promoted you to pilot. Valentina is going to be your navigator."

I glanced at Valentina, who nodded solemnly. "It's true. And Sophia will be mechanic. We've been assigned Larissa as our armourer."

I remembered Larissa from when I was injured. She was a small girl, with a face full of freckles, but she was remarkably strong for her size.

I felt the first tears sliding down my cheeks and let them fall. I had started the war wanting to be a pilot, but I'd been stuck as a navigator. I had hoped I'd be allowed to fly some day, but I'd never wanted it like this.

CHAPTER 27

"It's a great honour," Sophia insisted.

"Then you collect it," I replied, sighing. "It doesn't mean anything."

"What do you mean it doesn't mean anything?" Valentina asked, frowning over at me while she tucked her shirt into her skirt. She glanced down at herself, twisted left, then right and smiled slightly. In honour of the occasion, we'd finally been sent skirts, and heels. Heels! Antonina would have loved them.

I swallowed back tears and stepped into my own skirt. I'd had to tailor it a little to fit, but I hadn't shortened it as some of the girls had. I had simply taken the waist in so it didn't slide off my hips. If Marina Raskova had still been alive, she might have told them to stay up all night, if that was what it took, to let them back down. I remembered how she'd made Lillya Litviak fix her coat when she'd altered the collar. I preferred to leave my skirt to fall to just below mid-calf, but maybe I was too used to hiding behind trousers.

Well, Marina Raskova wasn't here and neither was Antonina, and so many others. I felt increasingly as though I was being surrounded by new, younger faces. Those faces looked at me with awe and respect, neither of which I felt worthy of. I was just Nadia from Moscow who happened to fly a Po-2 at the front and had been lucky enough to land a plane with one hand, at night. I was no more deserving of accolades than the next woman.

"I mean, it's just a piece of metal," I said. I couldn't resist swishing my skirt a little as well, in spite of my mood. My hair had grown out enough for me to fix it in place with combs and I'd been able to bathe that morning. I smelled nice and felt like a woman for a change. We might be warriors, but we were still girls at heart. Some days, it was difficult to remember that, but today we'd all look the part.

"Don't let anyone else hear you say that." Valentina looked up at me and grimaced. "You might get arrested for referring to the Order of the Red Star medal as 'just a piece of metal.'"

"I doubt I'm the first," I replied cynically. "Antonina's family will probably see hers that way. A medal won't bring her back."

Sophia and Valentina glanced at each other.

"It's not your fault she died," Sophia said softly.

"No, but I'm profiting from it with a medal." I hated the idea. I volunteered to fight and maybe die. I didn't volunteer to be held up as some kind of role model for my regiment. Surely they'd see that? General Vershinin would be about to pin the medal to my chest and he'd look at me. His eyes would look accusing.

"What is this silly girl doing here?" he'd demand. "You don't belong in a line of heroes, go back with the other girls and stop pretending." And he'd give the medal to someone more deserving.

"Lena Turova is getting one too," Sophia remarked, interrupting my unpleasant daydream with an almost equally unpleasant reality.

"She deserves it." Lena had seen another aircraft hit by anti-aircraft fire. It had lost part of its wings on one side and had sustained damage to the engine. The pilot had been having difficulty controlling the plane. It slewed to one side and wasn't responding to the right aileron. The plane was quickly loosing altitude and looked certain to crash. Instead of continuing on to the target, Lena had followed the aircraft behind enemy lines, technically acting outside of her orders.

The pilot of the other machine had to make a forced landing in an open field. With extreme danger to herself and her aircraft, Lena had landed her Po-2, picked up the two women from the other plane and evacuated the area before the Germans arrived to destroy the damaged aircraft. They'd come under heavy fire, but had managed to arrive back virtually unscathed. And Lena had simply dropped the women off and went back to work.

It was such a selfless act of such bravery we were all impressed. I might not like the woman, but I had to admit she had shown a lot of guts that night. She must have been terrified, but she'd typically shown no outward sign of any emotion.

"She didn't do anything you wouldn't have done," Valentina said generously.

"Perhaps." I sat down and pushed my feet into my new heels. "But I didn't, did I? I did nothing remarkable." And I was getting tired of talking about myself. It had never been my favourite topic of conversation.

"Anyway, today is about all of us, not just me," I reminded them sternly. I rose to my feet and teetered a little in the unfamiliar shoes. They had only a low heel, but felt very different from heavy army boots.

*****

In skirts and heels, we all stood a little taller, a little straighter, and a bit prouder. There was something about being clean and feminine that had a good effect on our egos. I stood in line with my crew, although the space where Antonina should have stood felt enormous and empty. Taking over for her as pilot, I had very large boots to fill, metaphorically speaking.

Although we'd shared the flying a lot of the time, the more daring and difficult flying had all been hers. I was a good technical pilot, but she had an instinct that made the plane seem almost an extension of herself. She'd also been a very capable squadron commander, who all of the girls had followed eagerly. I hadn't realised until now that the girls had idolised Antonina almost as much as they had Marina Raskova.

Her death had left such a gap in our regiment that her place had been left at the table for a full week before it had been packed away. Her funeral had been the most harrowing day I had ever lived through. If another person had asked me if I was all right, I might well have hit them. Of course I hadn't been all right. I'd cried all day and was too choked up to speak any words at her memorial. Sophia and Valentina, who had stood to either side of me through the whole thing, had been red-eyed and sniffing.

Sophia had spoken on behalf of us all, and everyone cried. And then we'd buried our friend and were expected to go on with life. Go on, we did, but not without missing her every day. I don't know who had cleaned her blood from the controls of the aircraft, but I was grateful not to have had to do that.

I raised my eyes as General Vershinin cleared his throat.

"When I was first told we'd be getting a women's regiment, I admit to being a little concerned. I wasn't sure you'd be tough enough for the work we'd give you. I knew you'd been trained by Marina Raskova herself, and that gave me faith in you. None of you have proved that faith to be wrong.

"Today, I bestow medals upon many of you, for great deeds of valour during this terrible war. But I also bestow a greater honour on you all. Today, you are no longer the 588th Night Bomber Regiment. From this day forth, you shall be known at the 46th Taman Guards Night Bomber Aviation Regiment."

A cheer went up from many of the women. I wiped a tear of pride from my eyes, but didn't much feel like celebrating.

"This honour I bestow today is for outstanding work in supporting our troops in the battles over and reclamation of the Taman Peninsula. Your exemplary bravery and sacrifice has been a great source of pride for our entire motherland. For this, I bestow the title of 'Guards' regiment. You join a very select group of elite divisions and regiments who hold this title. Continue your good work and remember, we will prevail!"

This time, I cheered a little, when everyone else did. I cheered because Antonina's sacrifice hadn't been entirely in vain. I applauded her efforts, and those of my sisters, not my own.

I stood in place until my name was called and the commander of the 4th Air Army pinned a metal to my chest.

"There you are, young lady," he said kindly. "I hope I didn't stick the pin in you." I knew he was perfectly aware he hadn't, but I gave him the smile he was after.

I realised all of the other recipients were beaming proudly, including Lena, while I had been scowling ungratefully.

"Thank you, sir," I said sincerely.

He lowered his voice and spoke so that only I could hear. "Don't doubt yourself. If you do that, then they win. Understood?"

I looked at him in surprise and swallowed hard. Had it been that obvious? Perhaps he was simply astute. No one achieved a rank such as his without being able to read and understand people, as well as tactics and logistics. If you couldn't understand the people around you, then how would you understand the enemy?

He raised an eyebrow at me.

"I understand, sir," I replied, trying not to trip over my own tongue. "We can't let them win."

"No, we can't," he agreed.

He gave me a nod and started to move on. Before he could, I said, "Excuse me, sir."

He stopped and arched an eyebrow at me.

"We're not princesses, sir."

He chuckled, obviously recalling Popov's remarks when he'd first met us. "No," he agreed. "No, you're not." He smiled at me and then walked on.

No, I thought, then perhaps I should stop acting like one. We had all lost friends and family. I had no right to act as though I were the only one. I squared my shoulders and wore my medal with pride, remembering it wasn't just Antonina's last flight that I got it for, but for many, many flights before that. It was for leading the search for the two planes that had collided and for my part in the liberation of Novorossiysk and the Taman Peninsula.

Maybe I wasn't a hero to myself, but if I inspired any of the younger, newer recruits, then I should be very proud. I might have to write to General Vershinin later for reminding me of that. A great leader, I had discovered, could motivate with just a few chosen words. Perhaps some day I'd learn to emulate people like Vershinin, Raskova and Antonina. In the meantime, I'd do the best I could to be me.

Five of the medals awarded that day were given posthumously. I couldn't hear any of their names, especially Antonina's, without a pang of grief. Hers would be sent in a little box, on a piece of velvet, to her family. Perhaps I would send them a letter. One of condolence, but also of thanks, for allowing us to spend this precious time with their daughter and sister. I'd tell them about the stories she shared with us, that she'd learnt at her grandmother's knee and how she'd talk about all of her family. I'd tell them how we loved her too and how much she'd missed and longed to go home to them. I'd tell them she was talented and strong and how she'd inspired me to be a better pilot. She'd been giving and generous and brave. And above all, she'd been my friend.

CHAPTER 28

I didn't recognise the writing on the flat, white envelope. It didn't look official -- it lacked a seal or any kind of embossing -- so I assumed yet again, it wasn't about my mother. Or at least, the government wasn't letting me know anything.

I knew it wasn't from Nikolai either, which made my heart sink, just a little. It had been months since I'd heard from him, and I missed reading his words. We were moving around so much -- and no doubt, so was he -- that it was difficult for mail to find us. There might well be several letters out there somewhere, trying to catch up to me. Personal communication wasn't really a priority during wartime, and these last few months had been particularly difficult, with intense fighting in the areas in which we'd been based.

We'd been transferred to a base near Krasnodar in the Kuban and both the weather and the terrain had made flying more hazardous. Sometimes it seemed as though both were a second and third enemy and were perhaps in collusion with the German army.

Since, as far as I knew, the fascists hasn't learned to rearrange land or control the weather, I just had to learn to work with or around whatever was thrown at us and hope winter would hurry up and arrive. Maybe this time it'd kill off those who remained after the last two winters.

"Are you going to stare at it or open it?" Valentina had taken up my old habit of sitting under the wing and pouring over the maps. She was looking up at me, but all I could see were her eyes.

"I thought if I keep looking at it, eventually I'd be able to see right through the envelope," I replied, grinning in spite of my sarcasm. "Actually, I was wondering who it was from. Do I know a Grigor Vlacic?" I frowned, trying to think back. It was no one from my childhood, that I could recall. That seemed another lifetime ago now, so I couldn't be certain. Perhaps he was from one of the men's regiments. There was probably a Grigor or two in those, but Vlacic didn't sound familiar.

She shrugged and almost hit her shoulder on the wing. "I don't know. It doesn't sound familiar to me either." Her eyes widened. "Maybe you have an admirer you don't know about?"

"I doubt it," I said.

"Open it," Sophia called from where she stood on the other side of the aircraft, patching a hole in the wing.

"Honestly!" Valentina exclaimed. "You must have ears like a...a...something that hears really well."

I heard Sophia laugh.

"Although," Valentina went on, "she has a point. Open it."

"Yes mother." I teased, sticking my tongue out at her. I heard her giggle and her face disappeared. I stuck my nail under the flap and tore it open. I didn't ever bother trying to open the envelope cleanly, once I'd decided I needed to see the contents. I had two older brothers; gentle wasn't in my upbringing. I unfolded the sheet of paper and started to read.

Dear Nadia,

I hope you don't mind me writing to you. I found some letters from you amongst Kolya's things...

I thought my heart had stopped for the longest time. Why would anyone be going through Nikolai's things? My mind immediately leapt to several conclusions, most of them ones I didn't want to contemplate. My heart in my mouth, I kept reading.

...so I knew you two must have been close. Kolya rarely talked about himself, but if you knew him, then you must have known that. He was a very private man, but in the last few months, he hardly said anything to anyone, so please don't be offended he didn't mention you to me. I didn't know him at all well, although I held him in the highest regard for his skills as a pilot.

I stopped reading and took a deep breath. This...Grigor, was referring to Nikolai in past tense, as though he'd...

There was a great battle, between our planes and those of the German Air Force. There were six of ours and forty-two enemy aircraft and I'm sorry to have to inform you we lost several planes that day. We did inflict great damage to the enemy, making several kills, which is always cause for great celebration.

We managed to find most of the machines and recover the crew or their bodies, but two pilots were hit and went missing. One of those was Kolya. We searched everywhere, even across enemy lines, but found no trace of him or his aircraft. Unofficially, he's listed as missing without a trace, but officially he's been listed as a deserter. If you know Kolya at all, you would know he would never have deserted. I might get in trouble for writing that, but I believe it to be true. It is unthinkable he would have walked away from us; he was too determined and dedicated for that. I'm sorry, but I can only think he must be dead.

Because you are a woman and a pilot, then you may want to hear about the other pilot who went missing. She was hit and we saw her plane fly off over enemy lines, with smoke coming out of its tail. I'm afraid although she's also listed as a deserter, she must also be dead. She was very brave and strong and courageous, as I'm sure you are as well. She was one of the best pilots I have ever seen. In fact, I hope you won't tell anyone, but I think she was the very best. Certainly her skills were far above my own, and I don't mind saying that at all. She was an exceptional woman. I think most of the men were in love with her. I know I was. Not that she would ever have looked twice at me. She will be greatly missed.

Her name was Lillya Litviak.

The letter dropped from my hand and floated down to land beside Valentina. She snatched it up and started reading.

"Oh no… Oh no, no, no." She came out from under the wing, her face wet with tears, sobbing softly. "Oh no, not Lillya!"

"Not Lillya what?" Sophia came around the side of the plane, wiping her hands on a dirty cloth. Valentina thrust the letter at her and sank back against the wing, devastated.

Sophia grabbed the letter just before it fell, read it and her face went pale. She blinked at it for a long moment and I watched her eyes move back and forth as she reread it. Her skin turned from white to a furious pink.

"Deserted, my old, fat, single, addled-headed aunt," she said angrily. "Neither of those two would have left their posts while there was a single German left fighting in this country. Neither of them. They would have fought until they had run out of bombs and bullets and rocks to throw. They would have…" The colour faded from her face again.

"Then they're dead," I said softly. The alternative was unbearable to even contemplate, especially for Lillya. Strange that although I felt shocked, and could feel my hands trembling slightly, I didn't seem to have any tears to shed for either of them. Perhaps I'd simply seen and heard and experienced so much death I just didn't feel it any more. I felt nothing, just cold and empty.

"Is there any more?" I asked, nodding toward the letter.

Sophia passed it back to me. I scanned the bits I'd read and already and continued with a bit down toward the bottom.

I am sorry to have been the bearer of such bad news and forgive me if this wasn't news to you at all. I hope I haven't caused you more pain. It may be they'll return to their regiments in due time. I wish this to be so. If they do, I will be sure to write to you, or have them write to you, to let you know they're alive.

Sincere regards

Grigor Vlacic

"It was nice of him to write," I said, folding the letter and putting it in my pocket. I put an arm around Valentina and let her cry on my shoulder. I was sad for her, she and Lillya had been good friends. Most of our regiment would feel her loss as acutely as Marina Raskova's, for many girls flew because they had seen Lillya fly before the war and had wanted to emulate her.

I was sad for Nikolai's friends, his regiment and his family. I would never see those soft brown eyes again, except in my dreams. However, I rationalised, it wasn't as though we knew each other all that well. We might have shared one meal and realised we weren't made for each other at all. Not that I didn't want him to be alive. I did, of course, but I wasn't going to let this break my heart.

I patted Valentina's back until her tears had dried up and then stepped back from her. "Are you ready? We're heading off shortly."

Our auxiliary field had been chosen and our target assigned. I had to resist the almost overwhelming urge to check and double check the maps and do the navigating myself. It was simply out of habit, not because I didn't trust Valentina. I had trained her myself. If she weren't up to the job then the fault would lie with me. So far, she hadn't done anything to make me think she was anything other than an exemplary navigator.

"Yes," she sniffed and wiped her nose. "We're bombing armoured vehicles again, to stop them from being able to transport troops. Tatiana wants us to go first and try for the searchlights and anti-aircraft guns."

She managed a vicious smile. I knew she loved attacking targets that were both helpful to the rest of the regiment and might kill a few of the enemy. For such a sweet girl, she took great pleasure in the death of the fascists. I didn't blame her. I might not be sweet, but I took some savage pleasure from inflicting damage on them as well. The girl who had sympathised with the young prisoner of war had hardened into a woman with concern only for her own people.

"Good." I nodded. "Go and get something to eat, then we can go and kill us some fascists."

I watched her and Sophia walk off. While they were gone, I started a quick letter to Grigor Vlacic in reply.

Dear Grigor,

Thank you for your kind letter and news. I hadn't heard either, so I appreciate you taking the time to write. I agree neither Lillya nor Nikolai would have deserted, but I don't care who sees me write that. They were good, honest, patriotic people who loved their country and would have given their lives for it, as I suppose they did.

Your regimental commander must have been terribly upset at the loss of two aircraft, they all seem to worry about that more than...

That sounded so cold. I scrunched up the piece of paper and started again.

Dear Grigor,

Thank you for your letter and kind words. I hadn't heard the news, thank you for breaking it as gently as you did. Their loss will be deeply felt. Please pass on my regards and condolences to your regiment and friends.

Ps, yes, everyone loved Lillya, but if she is dead, then she died doing what she adored and lived for.

Regards,
Nadia Valinsky

That was a little better. I folded the new letter and put it into my pocket with Grigor's. I'd send it in the morning, if I made it through the night.

CHAPTER 29

Valentina sneezed again.

"I'm so sorry," she said wearily. Her hair spread across the lumpy flat cushion that passed for a pillow. Her face looked pale against her red eyes and nose. "I can't even lift up my head."

I patted her hand but resisted getting any closer.

"It's all right, you have the flu. No one is going to blame you for needing to rest." I was surprised I hadn't gotten it yet, living in such close quarters. Sophia had it first, but she'd worked through it, refusing for a moment to rest. Some of the other women had had the most terrible bout of influenza, with one almost having to be evacuated to the rear. Luckily for her, transport had been delayed and she'd recovered sufficiently to stay.

Poor Valentina had gotten worse and worse last night and ended up sleeping through our last mission. I didn't mind navigating as well as flying, although I was worried she'd died on the way home.

"I felt like I might," she'd said afterward and staggered off to bed. Some enemies just can't be fought.

"I'll take Unka," I told Valentina. "She's been itching to get up in the air anyway and Evdokiia said she's ready." I smiled as Valentina groaned and patted her hand again. "Don't worry, she won't replace you. She'll get a couple of nights of excitement and then you'll be back, for duty."

She sneezed in response.

*****

"Ready?"

"Oh yes."

I wished I could have shared Unka's enthusiasm. She'd come to the front only a few weeks ago and had been training extensively with our training squadron. I knew she knew her stuff. But knowing that and trusting someone you hadn't worked with not to get you lost, were two different things. Of course I'd surreptitiously checked the map myself, so I had some idea where we were going, but I wouldn't let on to her. This was important to her and while I may choose to cover myself, I wouldn't insult her. Not obviously, anyways.

"All right then." I started the engine. I couldn't help but smile at the sound of it. There was something very soothing about that pop-pop. It was almost as though the plane was excited to get into the air. It might not have been built for fighting or dropping bombs, but it was constructed to soar up above the earth like a slow, ungainly bird.

Although we flew night after night, usually ten to fifteen times a night, I never got bored of it. The moon, the stars, the clouds, the wind, every time was subtly different and everything could change from one moment to the next. Clouds could roll in so quickly they could take us by surprise. We could be sailing along one minute and drenched with rain the next, or covered with flakes of snow. Some nights I desperately longed for a closed and heated cockpit.

The flight to the target was completely uneventful. Unka gave me directions and corrections and I followed them, occasionally having to wait for her to realise and speak up.

"Can you light me up a target please?" I asked through the intercom. I let the engine idle and glided toward the target.

"Yes, of course." I could almost hear her wriggling with excitement and smiled again. Her enthusiasm might not be contagious, but it was nice to hear. It was a shame there wasn't room on my crew to have her along permanently. Then again, I didn't want to think about 'war' and 'permanent' in the same sentence. Unka had a husband to go home to. They'd gotten married and then they'd both headed to the front. Had I ever been that idealistic? Maybe. I could vaguely recall it.

Unka tossed a flare over the side of the plane. The response from the ground was immediate. Searchlights swept upward, catching us in their glare. I was all but blinded, my eyes watering from the sudden bright light. I squinted to block out of some of it and side-slipped, trying to get us away, into the darkness where we could hide.

The searchlights went with us and the anti-aircraft fire followed. A shell slammed into a wing and the Po-2 shuddered.

"Hang on!" I called out, wincing as Unka squealed. I hoped it was with fright and not pain.

"I am!" she called back.

I turned the engine back on and pushed the controls forward and to the right, banking us hard and dropping our altitude until we were dangerously low. We were out of the lights, but I had to pull us up hard and level us out. Taking a deep breath, I turned us toward home, hoping the wing would hold out until we arrived. At least Unka would have a story to tell later.

*****

We'd been flying for at least five minutes when I saw something flashing past us. I heard Unka call out, "Nadia, there's another plane behind us. It's not ours!"

Yes, I'd figured that, since it was firing at us. I looked back and saw a Messerschmitt bearing down on us and our little biplane.

I did the only thing I could think of; I turned the engine off. The Po-2 idled so slowly the Messerschmitt flew right past us, unable to slow down enough to match our speed.

"There's another one!"

I switched the engine back on, just as fire from the second enemy plane hit us. Several more holes dotted our already damaged wing, spraying me with splinters of wood. I was grateful for my goggles then, as several large pieces bounced off.

"And another!" I looked out and in the light of an almost full moon I counted five.

Five against one? That didn't seem fair. And we were completely defenceless, armed only with our pistols. We'd never hit them across the distance and while they were moving so fast. I idled the engine again, hoping they'd fly past us and we could find somewhere to hide. We got about another hundred metres and our engine was hit. The plane shook violently and started to lose altitude.

I tugged desperately on the controls, but the nose only came up slightly, not enough to do more than slow our descent. I gave up on the idea of trying to get home and started looking for a flat place to land.

"Look for a field, a road, anything!" I called out desperately.

"I'm looking! It's so dark!"

Unka was right; it was too dark. I struggled to fight back my rising panic, but it was likely we wouldn't see what we were landing on until we were just about to land on it.

"Come on, there has to be somewhere," I spoke to myself, under my breath.

"There, there!"

"If you're pointing, I can't see you!"

155

"Sorry! West. There's a field."

There was a blackness that might have been a field. At this point, it was our best option.

The enemy passed by again, firing rapidly before soaring off into the inky sky. My heart pounded. We had to land and run before they came back to find us.

"Come on, come on." I twisted the controls and hoped the aileron on the remaining wing would respond. It did, banking us just enough to head us toward the field.

*****

I was dazed, but alive. I wriggled my fingers and toes. I could move, but everything hurt. I didn't think I had broken any bones. That was more than I could say about the poor Po-2. It would fly again, but only with new engines and it wouldn't be getting those while lying in a blackened field in the dark behind enemy lines. As much as I wanted to catch my breath, I knew sitting in my shattered plane was potentially deadly.

The thought that anyone might be on their way to kill us made me jump up and start gathering my things: a canteen full of water; my pistol and gloves; maps; a torch; and my compass. Even the aches all over my body wouldn't slow me down. My left arm and leg were both bleeding, but not enough for me to worry about it now.

"Come on," I turned to the rear cockpit to tell Unka to move.

What was left of Unka.

When the enemy had come around that last time, a bullet had scored a direct hit in her head. The back of it was all but gone; her blood splashed and smeared all over the cockpit.

My stomach churned; for a moment I thought I'd vomit. I swallowed it down and stuffed my belongings into a bag, except for the pistol. That, I put into the pocket of my coat. I leapt out of the plane and ran for the trees. In the distance I could hear engines and gunfire. I hated to leave Unka alone, but dying to keep her company was pointless.

I wanted to have torchlight, but I didn't dare to turn mine on. I might as well light a flare and yell to let the German army know where I was. There was just enough light from the moon to help me move around and avoid stones and exposed roots.

The only sound immediately close by was the rustle of some kind of animal, hopefully only a bird or a mouse. The idea of mice running around in the trees reminded me of Baba Yaga, which made me shudder. I kept my hands at my sides and away from tree trunks, although I knew they couldn't really hurt me.

After about an hour of stumbling around in the dark as quietly as I could, I found a place to hide in a hole under bushes. I dug it a little deeper and shoved myself inside. I paused then, taking a long moment to mourn my young navigator.

"At least you knew love before you died," I told her softly. She wouldn't be going back to her new husband after all. I sympathised with whoever would have to break the news to him. A widower at, what, eighteen? Of course he was far from the only one, but that wouldn't be any comfort to him, if he survived the war at all.

"When the war is over, or we regain this piece of land, I'll make sure someone comes back for you."

I waited for maybe an hour, but saw no one. If I was going to run, it would have to be now. I had maybe an hour or two before dawn to put as much distance between the crashed plane and myself as I could.

CHAPTER 30

As I walked, I silently thanked Marina Raskova for having chosen me to be a navigator. Using my compass and innate sense of direction, I knew exactly where I was in relation to my base and the auxiliary field. What I didn't know was where the enemy might be and if any might actually come looking for me. Maybe they wouldn't. Shooting down my plane was an effective method of stopping me from dropping bombs on them. My death probably wouldn't achieve much, except possibly their satisfaction and fulfilling their desire for revenge.

With those thoughts firmly in mind, I kept on walking.

"Do you want the whole German army to hear you?" A voice behind me made me jump and whirl around. I squinted into the briefest flash of light as it was turned on to a familiar face and then went dead.

"Lena?" Of all the people I thought I might see out here, Lena Turova wasn't even on my list at all. "What in the world…"

"I got shot down," she said, as if the answer was obvious. "Where is Valentina?"

"Back at base, she has the flu." For once, I was incredibly grateful to a virus. In the next moment I felt bad for preferring Unka's death to my friend's. "I was flying with Unka. She…she died." I hated saying that out loud, it made it so much more real.

"Inna too." Lena's regret was genuine; I could hear it the way her voice rose slightly.

"Oh no…" Everyone was going to be devastated by both of the deaths, but Inna Markova's especially. She'd been so kind and sweet to us all. "I'm so sorry…"

"Yes…" Her voice trailed away and I thought I heard her sniff. "You were a navigator, do you know where we are?" she demanded.

"Yes, that's why I was going this way," I replied, in as curt a tone as she'd

158

given me. "But we're going to need to find some thicker trees." I nodded at the faint orange glow off to the east. "Unless you fancy walking out in the open, in occupied territory in broad daylight?"

"No," she replied quickly. "Not really. Please, lead the way." It was the most humble I'd ever heard her and I realised with a start that she had no idea where we were, and she was scared. She needed me; that was new for us both. She was as self-reliant a person as I'd ever met.

*****

"Your boots are loud," she commented.

"What?" We'd only been walking for several minutes, but her speaking so suddenly took me by surprise.

"Your boots are squeaking. They're going to tell the Germans where we are. That's how I found you."

I looked down at my boots. They were squeaking a little bit.

"They'd have to have exceptional hearing," I commented.

"Take them off."

"I beg your pardon?" I frowned at her.

"I said take them off. Do you want to get shot? Or worse?"

I scowled at her, but sat down on a fallen tree to pull them off. When I rose and started walking, the boots now dangling from my hand, our passing was a lot quieter, but the ground was cold under my socks.

"Much better." She nodded

I wanted to throw my boots at her, but settled for another scowl instead.

We were walking for several hours at least when we found a place we could stop and rest. Bushes, dark and thick, surrounded it. Unless another plane crashed into us, then we should be safe for a while.

I took off my coat and used it as a pillow, then lay where I could see the sky through the thick leaves. My stomach rumbled and I cursed myself for not checking to see if Unka had brought any food.

"Here." Lena handed me a quarter of a sandwich. She took the same amount for herself and packed the other half away in a pocket for later. It was a little stale and covered in thick butter and nothing else, but it was food.

"Thanks." I nibbled slowly like the mouse in Baba Yaga and offered her my canteen. We both took tiny sips and then closed it tightly.

For a long while, we lay there in silence, listening to the breeze and the animals moving around nearby. Maybe I could shoot a rabbit with my pistol... No, the shot would give us away. Still, it would be so tasty.

"Why do you hate me?" Lena asked suddenly. I looked over at her.

"I beg your pardon?"

"The day we met, you seemed to hate me straight away."

I smirked. "I didn't hate you. I don't hate you now."

"Of course you do. Everyone does." In the shade I could see her face, her expression laid bare. She was insecure. The great Lena Turova cared what I thought?

"Well you're not exactly nice to anyone," I pointed out. "Everyone seemed to think you thought you were entitled to be a pilot."

"Do you think I wasn't?" Lena asked, frowning at me. "Have I not proven myself?" She sounded like a child desperate for some kind of validation; I just didn't understand why she'd want it from me. What did I know? I was nowhere near as experienced as she was. How was I supposed to respond to this?

I propped myself up on one elbow and looked over at her.

"Lena, you're one of the best pilots I've ever seen. You're talented and you're brave. But you know all of that. You remind us all every day."

She responded with a long silence, then, "Am I really that bad?"

"Do you really want an answer?"

"Nadia… " She paused and then sighed deeply, "I suppose I can be a little bit overbearing."

A little bit? "Maybe sometimes." I looked directly into her eyes. "I don't understand. Are you really that unsure about yourself? You're amazing. I'm surprised those Messerschmitts hit you."

Lena sighed and lay back to look up at the sky. "I had ten siblings, did you know?"

I shook my head. "No."

She took a deep breath. It was obvious to me that sharing like this wasn't something she was comfortable with.

"My parents were potato farmers. They probably still are. We were so poor that by the time the clothes I wore were handed down to me, they were made from the patches of old clothes. I had to fight my brothers and sisters for every morsel of food. The only way I ever got noticed was to be loud and pushy or to use my fists."

I pictured a younger Lena, her hands raised, ready to punch the bullies who harassed her. She wasn't a big woman by any means, but she was tough enough.

160

Lena continued, her voice low and humble in a way I'd never heard from her before.

"I left school the moment I was old enough and went to work in a factory, making tractors. The factory had an Osoaviakhim aviation school and I learned to fly. That was the only time I got noticed. Really noticed. I guess it was the first thing I had that made me feel proud of myself." She shrugged, making the leaves beneath her rustle. "That probably sounds pathetic."

"No, not at all." I was being perfectly sincere. Everything I'd seen since I'd met her made sense now. She wasn't so much being nasty as she was being defensive and that was because she was so insecure. I found myself reaching for her hand and squeezing it.

"I'm sorry you had it so tough. Maybe I assumed you'd be horrible because Sophia said you were full of yourself. That was wrong, I should have given you a chance."

"Sophia—she's so intimidating," Lena turned her face to look at me. "She's so confident. She's like a tank. Big and strong and invulnerable. She makes me feel so inadequate."

"Sophia would be very surprised to hear that. She's very soft on the inside." I hoped I'd get a chance to see her again. "But I'm not sure she gave you a chance either."

"Oh she did," Lena replied. "When we first met, she tried to be my friend. I mistook her sincerity for pity and pushed her away. You're right; I have been insufferable."

"Not insufferable," I assured her. "Just misunderstood. You're still my sister, the same as the rest of them. Just, we don't need to fight for food or wear patched clothing."

"I'd rather have the regiment as my family than my real family," she said vehemently.

"You don't miss them?"

She was silent for a while. Then softly, she said, "Sometimes."

We resumed our walk just as dusk was starting to settle. We were tired but determined.

We'd only walked for several minutes when we came to a road. It wasn't much of a road, really; more a dirt track through the forest.

"We must be close to our own lines," I said, peering between the bushes.

"I wish we—" Lena stopped talking, grabbed the back of my shirt and tugged me down behind the bushes.

Our recent understanding must have some an effect on me, because I didn't even think about protesting. I crouched down beside her, my lips pressed tightly together, not moving a muscle.

I was lucky Lena had reacted so quickly. A truckload of German infantry rounded a bend and slowly bumped past us down the track. Had I been standing, I would certainly have been seen.

I didn't dare to breathe. I had to resist the urge to swallow, just in case. I didn't even want to blink. This was the closest I'd been to the enemy since the young pilot had called us Night Witches. In spite of the failing light, it could see their faces, some smudged with dirt, most too young to be out here.

I felt like I was crouched there for hours, but they disappeared down the road in a minute or two. Then I let out a breath.

"Thank you," I whispered.

"Yes, well if they'd seen you, they'd have seen me." She shrugged. "Come on." We rose and continued on the road but staying in amongst the trees. Every time we'd snap a twig, my heart would skip a beat. I didn't want to come this far, only to get shot anyway.

"A bridge," Lena hissed, making me jump.

"What?" I peered through the trees and nodded. "You're right." The river it crossed looked too deep, too fast and too cold to cross by any means other then the bridge. But where there was a bridge, there would be one army or the other holding it. I grabbed her arm, tugged her down into the bushes and ducked down beside her.

"Ouch." She tugged her arm free and glared at me. "I'm perfectly capable of hiding, you know,"

I raised an eyebrow at her. I suppose our brief truce was over already. "Sorry, I just acted." I nodded toward the bridge. "Do we try to cross it or not?" There was no sign of anyone, from either side. "Maybe it's not held by anyone," I added doubtfully.

"We could try to run across before anyone sees us?" she suggested, looking back down the road. "Or we could stay here and watch and see…"

I didn't fancy either of those options. I chewed on my lower lip while I thought, trying to come up with a third choice. Before I could even consider any, I heard the crunch of boots behind us and the cocking of a gun.

I raised my hands to either side of my head and saw from the corner of my eye that Lena did the same.

"What are you doing here?" a male voice asked.

I lowered my head and nearly cried. He was speaking Russian.

Without turning around, I said, "We're both with the 46th Taman Guards Night Bomber Regiment." I might as well give our full title, not too many of the infantry had gained the honour of being a called 'guards'. "We were shot down."

"Ahhhh," he said, long and slow. "The notorious Night Witches. Well get up woman, get up. We better get you back to your regiment so you can bomb more Nazis, no?"

"Yes," I got to my feet and turned around. I'd never been so glad to see one of our men in uniform. "You hold the bridge?"

"Of course. And if you were Germans, you'd be floating down the river by now." He sounded so cheerful about it.

"Well maybe not so soon." He was joined by another soldier who looked us up and down. "But after a while you would. We've sent a few men down there. No women though. Only our girls are tough enough to fight."

Apparently they thought this was hilarious, because they both laughed loudly. I glanced at Lena and shrugged, although even the implied threat of rape was chilling.

"Come on, we'll find you a truck and get you home." The first soldier gestured toward the bridge with his weapon and smiled. Some men just got too much enjoyment out of war. At least we would be back with our regiment by dark. We might even be back in time to fly, if they could find us some more planes. Just because I'd been shot down didn't mean I'd be held back.

I nodded my thanks to the soldiers and started walking. Funny, they hadn't even asked why I wasn't wearing my boots.

CHAPTER 31

'As soon as possible', turned out to be two days. Our regiment had moved from the base where we'd left them and had been relocated elsewhere. It took an entire day for the radio operator to learn where they'd gone, in between taking and relaying orders. We were far from a priority, so I was grateful for their efforts. Once they found the 46th, it then it took an entire day to get us there in an ancient, rusty truck, bypassing positions held by the Germans. I was dreading them flying overhead and strafing our truck, but we saw no planes, either friendly or enemy ones.

We saw several other trucks and troop carriers, as well as soldiers on foot, but they were all ours and their trucks were all newer and better equipped than the one we rode in.

"It's kind of homely," I commented to Lena. "I'm used to ancient machinery by now."

She gave me her customary glare, but I knew now not to take it personally.

"You're right," she admitted. "I hated the idea of flying Po-2s at the start of the war, when the other regiments were in new Yak-1s and Pe-2s. It didn't seem fair somehow, that we were stuck with them."

"At least it wasn't just us. There are a few men's Po-2 regiments as well," I pointed out, wincing as we went over a bump.

"I know." She shrugged. "But they are reliable and sturdy and they take a lot before they crash. Although a Sturmovik would take more…" She looked wistful.

I sighed softly. She would probably never be satisfied; people like her never were. They were always looking for the next adventure, the next accolade. Bigger, better, faster, more.

"I'm surprised you haven't transferred to the 586th or the 125th." The 587th had been renamed the 125th M M Raskova Guards Day Bomber Regiment, in honour of its first commander. Its second and present commander was Valentin

164

Markov, a man who apparently hadn't been happy to take over command of a woman's regiment, but they had done admirably under him.

The 586th was the only women's regiment that hadn't gained the 'guards' accolade yet. They too had a male commander, Alexandr Gridnev, who also seemed a more than capable leader for the regiment.

Bombing during the day and aerial combat sounded much more dangerous and exciting for a woman like Lena, who wanted so badly to prove herself.

"I tried," she said flatly. "They won't let me go from ours. I'm making too great a contribution." She sounded disappointed with her own successes.

"Ah," I replied. "Too good for your own good, hmm?"

She narrowed her eyes at me, but I could see she knew I was teasing.

"I just want to be out there, being busy, killing fascists. There's nothing wrong with that."

"No, there isn't," I agreed. "That's all any of us wants. That and the war to be over." Personally, I was looking forward to a quiet life some day.

"What will you do, after the war?" I asked.

The question surprised her and she didn't answer straight away. "I'd like to stay in the Air Force, if they'll let me. I don't know that I'm cut out for anything else, and I can't imagine going back to an ordinary life." She lowered her eyes and I remembered what she'd said about her past. Working in a tractor factory would pall after all of the years we'd spent flying and fighting. Those girls who got a buzz out of it were going to find civilian life challenging.

"Although," she continued, "maybe I could be a flight instructor." She looked as though she were mulling over the idea and nodded. I could imagine her trying to train the next generation of Lillya Litviaks, Marina Raskovas and Raisa Beliaevas. They would keep even the most patient trainer on their toes, but Lena Turova would give them as good as she got.

"All of your trainees would be scared of you," I grinned.

That pleased her. "They would, wouldn't they?" She smiled and I could see her imagining that in her head, for her smile became almost wicked.

Then she looked over at me. "What about you? What will you do?"

Neither of us mentioned the possibility there might not be an after. We'd both just been shot down, we'd looked death in the eyes and we'd survived. We were far from immortal, but I felt a little luckier. Maybe I would see victory after all.

I shrugged. "I think I'd like to go back to university, finish my studies, become a teacher, get married, have children and forget I was ever a part of a war." That was more honest than I had even been to myself up until this point.

"Do you think you can really forget all of this?" She sounded scornful, but I saw empathy in her eyes when I looked over at her. She doubted it would be possible to move on with our lives as though we hadn't killed, seen death and nearly died ourselves, but she shared my sentiment.

"Probably not, but I can try."

Our reunion with our regiment was the second time I'd felt like a complete fraud. Because they'd been radioed ahead, they knew we were coming and everyone had turned out to greet us.

"So much for just quietly slipping back onto the base," I muttered, hearing the cheers of my sisters.

Lena chuckled. "Enjoy it. At least we know they're happy to see you."

"Both of us," I told her firmly.

My words were backed up by our regiment all but pulling us from the truck and making us both breathless with embraces. There were about three hundred of us now and I'm sure I was hugged by every one of them. Lena looked, and I felt, positively overwhelmed by it all.

"Welcome back!" Valentina squealed. She was looking much better than she had when I'd seen her last. She must have been glad she'd been sick, or it would have been her buried at the base of a tree.

Sophia hugged me so tightly, I thought she'd crack some ribs. "See, I told you she was alive."

"I never doubted," Valentina replied.

"I got a little present from the men's regiment," I told them softly, once we were alone. "They were very kind..." Out from under my coat I pulled a tightly bound package. I slowly peeled away the layers of cloth that had been someone's old shirt. It still smelled of sweat and fear. I didn't ask about the bloodstain on the chest.

Inside the shirt was a small bottle of a clear liquid.

"What did you do to warrant them giving you a bottle of vodka?" Sophia asked, almost accusingly.

"Well not that," I replied, slightly affronted by the suggestion. "I just told them about our regiment and they told me we once saved their behinds. We slowed the enemy just enough for them to move to a better position and they forced the Germans back. This was their way of saying thank you."

I opened the lid and held it up.

"So who wants some?"

"We're not supposed to…" Valentina looked worried. "We might get in trouble…"

"Oh come on, I just came back from the dead. Just this once can't hurt us, right?"

I held the bottle to my lips and took a swig. It burnt like fire all the way down to my stomach, but it felt strangely warming and relaxing.

"See? The world didn't end." I passed the bottle to Sophia, and Valentina even took a reluctant sip before passing the bottle back to me. I took another swig and another, as the three of us passed the bottle around and around. Before too long, it was empty and I felt as though I were floating.

"I've never been drunk before, it feels funny," I said.

"What? You're talking funny," Valentina giggled.

"Am not. I want food though. Let's go eat." I almost fell out the door to the dugout and for some reason that was the funniest thing that had ever happened to me. I started laughing and couldn't stop. My friends were giggling too.

"What's so funny?" I asked, blinking at them.

"I'm laughing because you're laughing," Sophia laughed. "Why are you laughing?"

"I'm not laughing. This is a war, it's not funny." Then I fell over and went on laughing. "People are dying. Friends are dying, I had to bury one. Nothing is funny." My laughter had brought tears to my eyes. I couldn't stand up. I tried, but my arms and legs wouldn't obey me and I kept wobbling and tumbling over. Luckily I was too drunk to feel any pain.

"Here." Sophia tugged me back to my feet. "I don't think alcohol agrees with you."

"I saw a turtle once," Valentina said once in a sing-song voice. "It lay on its back and kicked its legs in the air and couldn't walk or roll over. It was very funny. You looked like that!" Her giggles made me dissolve into more laugher and I had to lean against Sophia to stay upright.

"I'm a turtle!" I exclaimed. "I wanted to be a falcon but I ended up a turtle."

"You are a falcon," Sophia assured me. "One of Marina's Falcons."

"No I'm not," I suddenly felt a great need to argue. "Marina is dead and I have no wings. I crashed my wings into a tree and Unka died because she didn't have wings either. No wings for us. No wings, no wings!" I was almost singing the words.

"No wings," Valentina echoed.

"They'll get you new wings." How was Sophia still talking normally and making sense?

"You need to drink more," I told her, nodding my head so hard I could almost feel my brain rattle. "I need to drink more."

"No you don't," Sophia grabbed my hand before I could start off toward the men's regiment stationed alongside us at the base. We didn't have alcohol, but they would. "You need to eat."

"What? More herring and bread and rabbit stew?" I complained. Suddenly I was absolutely ravenous. "Yes, I'm hungry."

I staggered toward the mess and nearly fell again. Sophia grabbed me at the last moment and steered Valentina and I toward the mess hall.

"What in the world?" Lena Turova was leaving the mess and looked us all up and down. "Are you drunk?"

"Of course not," I slurred. "Hey, I thought you were really horrible, but you're all right." I went to give her a hug but she sidestepped and I fell against the wall. "Ouch. That wasn't nice."

"You stink," she told me, with such obvious disgust that I started laughing again. "You know that drinking is against our regimental rules."

"What, are you going to tell Evdokiia on me?" Suddenly the idea of getting into trouble — real trouble — made me feel a little more sober. I remembered the cabbage incident on the train and the way Marina Raskova had looked at me with such disappointment. I didn't want Evdokiia Bershankskaia looking that way at me, or Valentina. If she and Sophia got into trouble over this, it would be all my fault.

"Of course not," Lena replied. "But she's in the mess, so you should make yourself scarce until you're sober."

The old Lena wouldn't have hesitated to tell on us. She might have even found pleasure in doing it. But we'd come to enough of an understanding over the last three days that she actually had my back. I was relieved and gratified.

"Thanks," I murmured. "I owe you one."

"Oh yes," she agreed. "You do." She went to walk away, which was fortunate, because if she'd stayed where she'd been standing, I would have thrown up all over her boots.

"Never again," I swore, "never again."

CHAPTER 32

Lena was as good as her word and didn't tell Evdokiia about what we had done. Although, I suspected she knew, from the look she'd given me the next day. But since I came down with Valentina's influenza, my hangover was attributed to that. I spent a miserable week in bed, too exhausted to do anything but sleep. The rest did nothing to make me feel refreshed, in spite of my friends bringing me food and trying their best to be quiet around me.

Lena also hadn't been joking about getting a favour from me in return for her silence. When she was made squadron commander, she asked for me to become a flight commander in her place. Why she wanted me, I didn't know. Perhaps after our ordeal, she trusted me above the others. I certainly didn't want the job; commanding two other pilots and their aircraft was more responsibility than I could possibly want. I tried to refuse, but she called in my debt and I'd had to capitulate.

Until I had to do the job, I had no idea how much extra work was involved. I had to make sure three planes were ready instead of one. I had to make sure the other pilots had their orders and their navigators knew where to go. I had to make sure we all got to our auxiliary field. Lena certainly hadn't done me any favours by choosing me. Maybe she inflicted this on me because she really didn't like me after all.

"What?" Valentina asked, interrupting my train of thought. "You're frowning."

"Hmm? Oh, I was just thinking. Is everyone ready?" I looked over at the two other Po-2s and their enthusiastic young pilots. I wasn't sure I'd be so happy if I was under my command, but they seemed to think it was some kind of honour. Fraud number three. How many more would I have to my name before the war ended?

I gestured for one of my young pilots to go first, as we'd organised. The other would follow her and we'd bring up the rear. This way, I could keep an eye on them and see how well they were hitting the target. They'd been well trained out here at the front, so this would be just another mission. I wasn't nervous about them or their flying. I was scared I'd do something to fault them, like get shot down again.

I reasoned I wouldn't want to follow me if I couldn't stay in the sky. Although so many of us had been shot down there were many commanders who had been through the same thing. At least I'd survived.

I watched the first plane taxi and take off, followed by the second. The minutes ticked by, one, two. We took off on three. The night was cloudy and cool for mid-summer. We might get a storm later, or some rain. That might cool the days down a little.

Everything was pitch dark as we approached the target. I knew there were several other planes in front, but I couldn't see them. There were no searchlights or sign of lights on the ground.

"Are we in the right place?" Valentina asked through the intercom.

"Um, you're the navigator, sweetie," I reminded her. I had been thinking the same thing though.

"This should be it," she said uncertainly.

"Oh my…"

Out in front of us, a fireball lit up the night like a firework.

"What is that?" Valentina asked. I could feel her peering out over my shoulder.

"I'm not sure…" A couple of minutes later, another explosion lit up the sky and I realised what I was seeing. A fighter plane was silhouetted by the light of a Po-2 they'd just attacked. The fire had been my regiment's planes burning.

"They've got fighters shooting at us!" Valentina exclaimed. My heart sank. No wonder there had been no searchlights, they'd been lying in wait for us, ready to shoot us out of the sky.

Another explosion followed and another one shortly after.

"Get out of here!" I called via the radio, forgetting protocol in my haste to warn the plane in front of me and those behind. I banked sharply and pushed the Po-2 for everything it had, trying to put as much distance between the fighters and us as I could.

I held my breath, sensing them out there behind us, hunting us in the darkness. The Po-2 was so slow and flimsy and flew so low they seldom appeared on enemy radars. I took us down even lower, too low for them to follow. I hoped we were too low for them to see, but not low enough for us to hit a tree.

My heart was racing; dread and the all too familiar feeling of having done this before making my hands tremble slightly when I most needed them to be steady. I swallowed and took deep breaths, trying to suppress the growing feeling of panic that was rising in my chest.

"Can you see anything behind us?"

"No, nothing." The fear in my navigator's voice did little to calm my nerves. "It's just black…" The darkness that was hiding us might be hiding the enemy as well.

"Just a few minutes more…" Hopefully the regiment was already evacuating the auxiliary field. If we hadn't needed to refuel, I might have headed straight back to base.

Those few minutes quickly became the longest few minutes of the war. My heart was in my mouth the entire time. My stomach churned and I hoped I would manage to hold on and not vomit in the cockpit.

The feeling of the wheels touching grass was the single sweetest feeling I could remember having. It was even more wonderful than the realisation the infantrymen who had found Lena and I had been our troops.

The wind rushed by as we slowed. It was warmer down here, almost hot. I brought the aircraft around and drew to a stop.

"Nadia?" Sophia's voice in the darkness sounded terrified.

"Yes, we're here, we're fine." It was remarkable how quickly she'd learnt to identify the sound of the new engine when our plane had been replaced after the crash. It was like a sixth sense that never failed her.

If felt her rush out of the darkness and climb onto the wing. "Where are the others?" she asked, her voice full of high emotion. "Did you see?"

"I saw."

Only now it hit me, what exactly I had seen. Four of our planes, four of our regiment. Eight of our sisters, gone. Burnt into nothing before my eyes and those of us all.

"It was horrible," I said, disbelief giving way to sorrow. I rubbed my temples with my fingertips, feeling a huge headache coming on.

One of our administration officers trotted past, stopping only long enough to call out, "We're packing up and going back to base. No one is flying out there with them in the sky."

"No, of course not." Eight women. It was hardly comprehensible. I didn't want to comprehend it; I didn't want to think about it. The Germans had used a new tactic against us and it had shattered our regiment. How were we supposed to go up there now, with fighter planes ready to shoot down defenceless aircraft before they even dropped their bombs?

"Just…get us refuelled," I said wearily. "We need to get out of here."

Sophia hurried to do as I'd asked and I listened for the other planes landing. Senia, one of the pilots in my flight, brought her Po-2 home several minutes after me, but Maritsa would never return. I couldn't bring myself to ask or acknowledge who the others were until we'd arrived back at our base.

We'd been ordered to a debriefing and we all went, pale-faced and shaking. Many of the girls were weeping, handkerchiefs scrunched up in their hands. My headache was pounding now and I wanted my bed, but I slipped into a chair.

Evdokiia Bershankskaia looked tired and drawn from the strain of leading us and losing so many of us. She must have been wishing she'd continued to turn down Raskova's offer to lead. If she'd known then what she did now, she might have dug in her heels until they inflicted the job onto someone else. I sympathised with her position; I wouldn't have wanted it either. Maybe I should have made Lena pick another favour.

I glanced around the room, but didn't see her. Then it hit me like a truck driving into me at full speed. One of the women killed tonight was Lena Turova. I clapped a hand over my mouth and gasped into my palm. Her hopes and dreams and high aspirations would now come to nothing. She'd been blown apart in her plane, leaving us with not even a body to cry over. Nothing but a place at the table.

I should have felt tears sliding down my cheeks, but I had none. Just the emptiness in my chest. I had no sobs, no rivers of tears. I felt cold all over, inside and out.

"Who else?" I heard Valentina ask softly.

"Klavdia and Katya," Evdokiia replied, weary and shattered.

It felt like the war was gradually picking off all the people I had known since Engels, and even before. Marina Raskova; Lillya Litviak; Nikolai; Anya; and now these women. And I could still not find any more tears to cry. Was this what happens to soldiers? They saw and did so much their hearts just turned to stone. When I died, if they cut me open, they'd just find a piece of rock. Would it shatter if I exploded too?

"What do we do tomorrow?" I asked. Everyone turned to look at our commander. Many had wet faces and red eyes, but one or two women looked as clinical as I felt.

"Yes, what do we do? We don't stand a chance against them, do we?" one of them asked.

Lena's response would have been that they should have given us Sturmoviks or Pe-2s, and I would have agreed. Either would have given us the firepower to fight back. It might have been satisfying to shoot down an enemy plane or two.

"Parachutes wouldn't have helped," Sophia remarked. We'd been over and over this in the last few years. Parachutes took up extra weight and we flew too low for them to be of use, and tonight they would have saved no one. The attacks were too swift and the planes had burnt too quickly. Although, maybe one or two would have survived...

"We'll have help," our regimental commander said firmly. "We'll have an escort of fighter planes the next time we go up."

Good, I thought to myself. *Let them be the target.* It might be easier if we flew them ourselves, but we had no time to retrain in them anyway.

"Nadia."

I brought my eyes up to hers, thinking: *Don't say it, just do not say it.*

"You're taking over as squadron commander."

I wanted to hit my forehead into the table, hard and repeatedly, until those words became a bad dream or until she took them back and inflicted the supposed honour onto someone else.

"Yes ma'am," I said instead. I could feel Valentina and Sophia looking at me, but I'd lost an aircraft today and felt far from worthy of the promotion. Yet again, I felt like a fraud. I was losing track of how many times that was now, but I doubted this would be the last. When was everyone going to realise I was just Nadia Valinksy, the student teacher from Moscow?

"Congratulations Junior Lieutenant," Sophia said. The look I gave her should have melted snow, but she looked unrepentant.

CHAPTER 33

"Junior lieutenant, there's someone out there."

I had a difficult time trying to figure out just what bothered me more: being addressed by rank or the fact she was right. For the two months I'd held the rank, I'd been trying to play it down, but Lydia Bershova was new to the regiment and insisted on addressing everyone correctly, with their formal titles, as if she were seventeen and we were in our forties. She was eighteen and I had just turned twenty-three.

Truthfully, I'd almost forgotten my birthday. It just didn't seem all that important out here. It wasn't as though anyone could make a cake or have a party. At most, we might sing some songs and dance, but I was in the mood for neither. Luckily all I got was a candle Sophia had scrounged stuck into a slice of bread. I was touched by the gesture. Anything more would have been a waste.

"Less is more," Valentina had said cheerfully. "Let's hope it's cake and the war is over by the next time you have a birthday."

It was now spring of 1944 and we'd been at the front for two long years. In spite of our victories and the German's retreat from some of the locations we'd forced them from, the war was still well and truly on. The fighting had been intense all spring, with the front line moving back and forth like the tide.

"I'll settle for still being alive," I remarked. Some days I was sure it wasn't the fascist army that would kill me, or the nine aircraft and twenty-six women I had under my command. Some days it felt as though I had finished my teacher training and was surrounded daily by children; children who flew and were armed. At least their weapons were never aimed at me. Well, not that I could see anyway. I'm sure they talked about me behind my back and thought me cold and heartless. Maybe I was, but only because the war had made me that way. Perhaps it would be better if my mother was dead. Better that than seeing the person her daughter had become. Maybe if I survived, I wouldn't go home, just in case. Let everyone think me dead. Would it even matter?

I turned to look at Lydia.

"Can you see who?" I asked.

She shook her head slowly, wisps of dark brown hair coming loose from her braids. She would have been mortified if I'd pointed them out and would have fixed her hair immediately. I didn't though, because I didn't care how her hair looked. Just because she was a stickler for rules and protocol didn't mean I was. Most of us weren't anyway. The fact that she'd see her hair later and think it a mess made me sigh out loud.

"I'm sorry ma'am, I just can't see…" Lydia looked so worried she'd let me down I almost sighed again.

"No, no, of course you can't." I wanted to remind her to call me Nadia, but I had already done that, several times, and nothing had changed her habit of addressing me by my rank, or as 'ma'am.'

I turned to Sophia. "Any word on troop movement in the area?"

She shrugged. "Only that the enemy and our troops are both really close to us and to each other. I'm surprised they haven't moved us to another base yet."

I nodded my agreement. With both armies so close, we were on edge day and night. The thought of accidentally bombing our own people was horrifying. I suspected if it meant making an impact on the enemy, we might just have to risk doing that. As far as I knew, it hadn't come to that, but they probably wouldn't tell us anyway.

I stood still and gestured for everyone to do the same while I listened. There, in the trees, I could hear movement. No one spoke, but the leaves shifted and twigs cracked under boots. The idea of Germans creeping through the bushes to attack us sent shivers down my spine. It was something they hadn't done before, but our bases had always been at a greater distance from them than now. Killing us on the ground would be like shooting the proverbial fish in a barrel, especially if we couldn't take off. I glanced skyward but heard no engines that might signify the approach of enemy planes. Although I knew very well how aircraft could sneak in over a target.

I pulled out my pistol. Unless we were ordered to evacuate by air, I'd just be ready to defend myself. I glanced around at my squadron and gestured for them to do the same. We only had a few bullets between us; we'd have to make every shot count.

I chewed my lip. Should we advance on the tree line or hide behind the planes? No, we needed to stay away from the planes. They'd be a huge target as it was, but we'd need to defend them against the enemy if we could. There were many more of us than there were aircraft, so our homeland would need them more. A chilling thought, certainly. I'd do my best to make sure that as many of my girls made it out as possible.

So no hiding then? Should I have us advance? This kind of thing hadn't been taught to us before and I hated that this decision was on me. Evdokiia was working with the training wing and the other two were across the airfield. I could radio for orders, but it might be too late by the time anyone made a decision.

"Nadia?" Sophia asked softly.

Her too? Too many people were relying on me and my judgment. I gestured for them all to stay back and I started forward alone. I'd get shot first, but it would give my squadron time to act. Maybe it was foolish, but my life for theirs seemed a simple decision to make.

I held my breath as I reached the edge of the trees. The boots were getting closer; I could almost feel their movement through the undergrowth. Now, I would have liked Baba Yaga and her hand-eating tree, if only to suck a few of the enemy away.

I raised my pistol and heard a squadron of women cocking theirs behind me. I hoped their aim would be true. Death by friendly fire was another way I didn't want to die. My heart hammered in my throat. I could see movement in the trees now, uniforms almost blending in with the foliage.

My finger tightened on the trigger. I had it aimed at head-height. I was taking no chances that the first man out of the trees would be alive and able to return fire.

The leaves were pushed aside and a man stepped out, one hand on his weapon, the other in the air.

"Don't shoot, we're on your side."

With a loud exhale of relief, I lowered my pistol. "You're lucky, I almost put a bullet in your head."

He grinned at me; cheeky, cocky man. "I would hate to be shot by a girl. That might be worse than being killed by Germans."

"We could make sure you find out, if you like?" I said dryly.

He laughed and turned to wave his men forward. "No, no, we like life too much. But if I change my mind, I'll let you know—?" He prompted me for my name.

"Junior Lieutenant Nadia Valinsky." I realised with some amusement that I outranked him. "Private?"

"Sergey Zhikin." He didn't look bothered about being a lower rank than a woman. "Our CO was shot. So was his. We need to get back to our division. But we could stay for the night…" He looked the girls up and down and I had to resist the urge to punch him in the nose.

"You can use our radio to contact your division," I told him. "It'll be up to them whether or not you stay. This way." I gestured for the men to follow me

Zhikin looked a little put out at my response, but I simply turned on my heel and walked toward the base headquarters. I didn't have time for sulky boys, even ones as handsome as this. The other girls could flirt and swoon and dig out their lipstick to impress the men; it didn't interest me.

What was the point of becoming attached to someone who might not be around the next day? Or falling for someone, only to have them die? Or letting someone fall for me, and then dying myself? Maybe when the war was over, if I survived, I could make a quiet life with someone who wanted the same.

A few of the girls had attachments to men from the men's air regiments, as I had had with Nikolai. Those men would probably keep flying after the war, putting themselves in constant danger. I didn't want that for myself or any children I might have some day. The thought of a normal life was such a long way from here and now I almost laughed at myself for thinking it. What would 'normal' even feel like?

"I hope they don't hurry off too soon," Valentina whispered, having hurried to catch up to me.

I snorted softly. "You're as bad as…never mind."

"What?" I didn't look, but I could feel her staring at me. "You were going to say Antonina?"

I was.

"Of course not," I replied hastily. "I was going to say you're as bad as a giggly schoolgirl."

"Antonina always said you were a horrible liar," she snapped at me. I looked at her in surprise but she'd walked off toward the mess hall. She'd never been cross with me. Although, perhaps I'd never spoken to her like that.

"Valentina!" I called out after her. She didn't stop or even look back.

I sighed. Sometimes it was easy to forget that this war was having an impact on us all. I'd become so good in wallowing in self-pity that I'd missed seeing one of my closest friends was struggling as well. I swore to myself I'd talk to her later. In fact, I'd make sure my entire squadron was doing all right. I did care about them, but I couldn't blame them for believing otherwise.

I turned to Zhikin and pointed out our radio room. The radio operators would take over from there.

"Feel free to use the mess hall while you wait." Not that they needed permission from me, but the infantry had been good to Lena and I, so returning the favour was the least I could do. They wouldn't be leaving here with a bottle of vodka from me though. The thought still made my stomach turn. How the men drank a daily ration of the stuff was beyond me. If it was supposed to make them feel better, it hadn't worked for me. Unless of course in thinking a slow death at the hands of the enemy might be preferable to a hangover. In which case it worked admirably.

"Thank you, pretty lady." Sergey Zhikin gave me a bow and a smile, dimples showing in his boyish cheeks. "Maybe I'll see you at dinner then?"

"Probably not, I have work to do." I ignored the look of disappointment in his eyes. There would be no point in me feeling bad for letting him down. He'd be gone tomorrow and forgotten, and he'd forget me, except maybe to tell stories of the way they'd come upon the 46th and had almost been shot by women. No doubt they'd be telling that story for years.

CHAPTER 34

The pain was excruciating, all down the left side of my body, from the edge of my cheek to the part my calf not covered by my boot. For a long while, that was all I was aware of. I thought I might die, I hoped I would, if only to end the agony. It could have been minutes, it could have been days I lay like that, trying bear the pain and will it to alleviate.

When I finally managed to compose myself and start to take stock of where I was, I found I was lying on something hard and uneven. That could have be anything from my bed on the base, to the ground. I moved my right shoulder and winced. I didn't think it was broken, but I'd have some nasty bruises. My head ached, but it wasn't the ache I got from stress. It hurt as though I had hit it, or had been hit. I frowned, trying to remember, but that only caused more pain.

I opened my eyes a crack. It was dark. I could see the stars overhead but nothing else. In the distance, I could hear the crack of weapons fire. The night smelled of gunpowder and something metallic; I think it might have been my blood in my mouth.

I tried to move but my body wouldn't obey me. Beneath me, the earth shook and a flash lit up the night sky. I closed my eyes to shield them from the sudden glare and passed out.

When I woke again it was still night. The pounding in my head was slightly less, and the pounding of weapons had stopped. The ground was still, but the air stank. The breeze carried the scent of smoke and that same metallic smell.

I strained my ears, but the silence was profound.

I opened my eyes and turned my head. Over toward the east, I could see the first rays of sun just starting to appear. I knew I couldn't just lie here, but my mind was addled and sleepy and I couldn't remember why. I just wanted to sleep. Maybe if I slept, the pain would be gone when I awoke.

It wasn't. The sun was just peeking over the horizon, orange sunrise filtered by smoke. I remembered smelling smoke the last time I awoke too. Good, I was starting to remember. I was Nadia. I was, I am, from the 46th Taman Guards Night Bomber Regiment. We had just been visited by the men from the infantry we'd almost shot. They'd stayed the night. Was that last night, or weeks ago? I was forgetting something important, but it wouldn't come to me.

I wanted to go back to sleep. It was morning, time to rest. I forced my eyes to stay open. I turned my head to the side. Burned wood, mangled mess of something…my plane, my Po-2. Those men had come and gone, but that had been months ago. I'd caught one of my girls kissing one, after he'd washed his face. It wasn't against the rules, so I'd simply given her a stern look. At least he'd washed his face. I had no idea why that was important, but I'd remembered it.

And my stern look. When had I become one of those people I'd feared at the start of the war? The people who could scare me or make me ashamed with just a look? I'd been so intimidated, but I never thought I'd be intimidating. I never wanted to be like that.

War changes people.

I forced myself to focus. My aircraft, was it burnt? I lifted my head but it swam and hurt, I had to lower it back down immediately. I didn't need to see; I could smell it anyway. That metallic smell was me, my blood, not just in my mouth but on me, on my uniform. Blood was difficult to wash out. I might need a new uniform. Why were my thoughts so jumbled and random?

The sun was a little higher in the sky. My head didn't hurt as much. I forced it to lift up off the ground and stay up. I propped myself up on my right elbow and ignored the wave of dizziness that threatened to engulf me. I had to get up. If I didn't, I would die.

It took me at least ten more minutes to sit up. My flight overalls were singed, the fabric sticking to blistered skin. Dirt and dust stuck to it as well. I'd need to get it washed and dressed as soon as possible, or it would become infected. At the least, I'd have an ugly scar. Lots of scars, I amended, looking down at the side of my leg. It wasn't as bad as my arm and shoulder, but it didn't matter. I was alive.

I squinted over at the wreckage of my plane. Another ruined plane, this time in an open field. I staggered to my feet and looked around. There, about one hundred metres away, was a stand of trees. It wasn't much, but I needed some cover. My mind was begging me to lie back down and sleep, but I made myself walk.

I needed to run. The back of my mind was yelling at me to move, but my body wouldn't respond. I could only manage a few steps at a time. Everything hurt, and my head was pounding again, worse than before. I looked down and watched myself take every step, one after the other. I willed my feet to keep moving. Somehow they obeyed, shuffling, until I reached the trees.

I collapsed under them and gave in to the desire to sleep.

*****

When I woke again, I wasn't alone. I could hear boots approaching slowly, crunching on dry twigs and dirt. They weren't in a hurry, nor were they making any effort to be quiet. I opened my eyes and squinted against the glare of daylight. The ground under my head was uneven and I had a twig under my cheek. I must have passed out if I'd been sleeping like that.

"Valentina?" I lifted my head, only to have it shoved back hard against the ground. My vision swam, overwhelmed by pain. Suddenly the night before came back in stark clarity.

We'd been over the target and had dropped our bombs. They had detonated on cue, but the searchlights had shown our position. I had banked the plane out of the searchlights, but they'd taken a shot, guessing at the direction we'd been about to go. I couldn't anticipate their move and their aim had been true. A shell had hit one of the wings, tearing the canvas to shreds.

Knowing the plane was about crash, I ordered Valentina to bail out. We'd only recently been issued with parachutes and I hoped we were about to justify the increase in weight the plane had to endure to carry them.

"Not without you," she had insisted.

"I'm ordering you, out." I had said. I pushed the Po-2 for everything it had, but it wasn't enough. We hadn't crossed our lines before Valentina had been forced to jump. I only hoped I'd given her enough altitude for her parachute to open before she hit the ground.

By the time she was clear of the aircraft, I was overcome by smoke and flames. I had to convince myself I had saved my friend, so my death wouldn't be entirely in vain. I felt a searing pain in my arm and watched in morbid fascination as my uniform burnt and my skin bubbled and blistered beneath it.

That was the last thing I remembered. The Po-2 must have hit the ground, nose first, throwing me clear and slamming me into the ground. That saved my life. I would been incinerated inside my plane, instead of lying dazed beside it.

I cracked open my eyes and reached for my pistol. Before my hand was even close to my holster, a booted foot stepped firmly on my wrist. Another kicked me hard in the ribs. My eyes shut as I doubled up, trying to protect myself from further attack.

A shadow fell over me and the face of a German soldier was mere centimetres from mine. While his companion pinned my wrist, he reached for my pistol and tucked it into his own pocket. I felt the first stirring of despair in my chest. I needed my weapon. If not to use it on them, then I needed it to use on myself. A woman captured by the German army… I didn't dare to think what they might do to me.

"Hände hoch!" The one with his boot on my wrist lifted it and gestured with his weapon, indicating that I should get up.

"I don't understand," I lied. Maybe they would kill me now, for being obstinate.

He grabbed my arm and pulled me to my feet. I bit my lip to keep from crying out in agony. Tears trickled down my cheeks from the pain and humiliation. His fingers stuck to my skin. His face was filthy and unshaven, but it was the hatred in his eyes I'll never forget.

He shoved me forward with his open hand and I staggered a step. My legs almost gave out beneath me and my flying helmet slid down my right cheek and onto the ground. I watched it roll a few paces and come to a stop against a stone. My hair tumbled loose and fell now to my shoulders.

One of the men muttered something in surprise and grabbed a handful of my hair in his fist. I shook my head slightly, not understanding what he was saying. Valentina would have understood. She had learned German in school and had had a flair for it. I could guess though; he was surprised to have captured a woman. Until now, they must have assumed I was a male pilot. I cursed myself for allowing my hair to grow back.

It was folly, I quickly realised. No matter what, I wasn't going to be well treated anyway, because I was the enemy. The fascist tugged at my hair and then shoved me forward, forcing me to walk in front of them. I considered running, encouraging them to shoot me, but I lacked the energy. And strangely, considering I'd stared death in the face a few times now, I decided I wasn't ready to die. Instead, I would wait. I would be compliant and then escape.

I was shoved into a small enclosure like an animal. It smelled of human filth and misery. Several hundred pairs of eyes stared at me; some with curiosity, some with pity, but most with the disinterest born of having seen too many people added to their miserable milieu. Every one I saw were men, all filthy, burnt from the sun and as thin as Baba Yaga's cat. Some were lying still on the ground, flies buzzing around open wounds. Others sat and looked at nothing, hopelessness in their posture and eyes. They must have once been proud people, but now they were broken and waiting to die.

That would not be me, I swore to myself. No matter what happens, what they do to me, they will not kill me and they will not break me. I looked for the most cognisant prisoners and sat down near them. My arm and shoulder hurt so badly I wanted to scream, but I held my head proudly and bit my lip. I was a Night Witch. The women of the 46th did not give up and we did not give in. I would escape and return to my regiment. Then I would kill the men who imprisoned me.

CHAPTER 35

I was taken from that open compound after a single day and loaded into the back of a truck. It smelled of animals, excrement and urine, all baked in merciless heat. I was being transferred with several other prisoners. I realised, to my surprise and horror, I recognised a few of them. I had seen them around various bases and had served alongside one or two of them.

"You're Air Force too?" I asked the man beside me.

He nodded grimly. "Gunner," he said simply and held out his hand. "Lisov." I shook his hand. "Nadia."

When he looked quizzical, I added, "From the 46th."

"Ahh, night bombers? The women's regiment."

I suppose, since the other two regiments had acquired men during the war that yes, the 46th could be referred to as the women's regiment. I mightn't have thought of it as such, but I didn't bother to correct him.

"Where are we going?" I asked, looking out the side of the truck.

Lisov shrugged. "No idea. They ship people out all the time. No one ever comes back to tell where they were taken."

"How long?"

"Since I was captured?" He sighed. "About a month."

"You're going to escape though?" I asked.

He gave me a long, searching look and then a faint smile. "I haven't given up. It just gets more difficult every day. These people don't think of us as human, they treat us like animals. It's how they justify starving and beating us. You'll see, soon enough. They seem to take pleasure in reminding us we're nothing."

"We're not nothing," I protested. "We're airmen and airwomen." If anyone was subhuman, it was our captors. Surely my people weren't treating their prisoners like starved cattle? I grimaced slightly. All right, I wasn't naive anymore, but they were the invaders, the transgressors. They got what they deserved, especially the

184

suffering and death.

Lisov shook his head wearily. "No, we're not nothing. Keep remembering that, no matter what they do to you." He gave me such a haunted look I didn't dare to ask.

I nodded and whispered, "I'll remember. If you swear to do the same."

He almost looked bemused at this. "The new ones always want to save the world."

Once, a long time ago, I might have stuck out my tongue at him. I had outgrown such a childish action though and this wasn't the time or the place. Instead, I simply frowned at him and then shrugged.

"Someone has to," I said. "Or we all might as well give up right now." That was something I wasn't willing to do, even if I had to escape alone.

*****

There must have been thousands of prisoners in the camp. The stench was overwhelming and turned my empty stomach. I had almost passed out again in the truck. Lisov and a young pilot helped me off and were immediately ordered to one side, with all of the other men. I was shoved to another. A guard grabbed the back of my uniform and all but dragged me to a small wooden hut set slightly apart from the others. He unlocked the door with an old key and pushed it open. It creaked in protest from what must have been years of overuse by now. He put a hand on my back and shoved me inside.

The door slammed shut behind me. I heard the snick of the lock being engaged again and boots walking unhurriedly away.

Then I was alone.

The small room consisted of nothing but walls and a tiny camp bed; the latter short and narrow. There were no windows; light came in through tiny cracks in the walls. I shuffled over to the cot and sat down gingerly. It sagged almost to the floor and several fleas leapt clear. Regardless, I lay down, tucking up my feet so they wouldn't hang over the end. I turned and lay on my good arm; I needed the rest. I'd need the energy for my escape.

There was a crack at eye-level, but all I could see was another hut a few metres away. Occasionally someone would move past and I'd watch them, following them with my eyes and willing them to come and let me out. If they knew I was there, they didn't give any indication.

Hours passed and I slept. Someone must have come to the door, because I awoke to find a cup of water that didn't look very clean and a piece of mouldy bread sitting on the floor just inside. I cursed myself for sleeping. Every time the door opened, it was a possible chance to escape and I'd missed the first one. I was determined not to miss another.

I rose, although my whole body ached. My injuries hurt so badly I wanted to scream, but I saved my energy. I walked the few steps to the very meagre meal and quickly picked it up, watching the door in case this was some kind of trick. The door stayed shut, so I darted back to the cot.

"And now, out comes the grey mouse to save me from Baba Yaga," I muttered to myself. But no grey mouse appeared and I ate all of the bread myself. The water wasn't nearly enough to either slake my thirst or wash my burns. I did hesitate for a while, thinking the wise thing to do would be to conserve it for later. However, once I took a sip, I couldn't stop. I quickly drank it and wished for several litres more.

The pain overcame me then and I slept for a while, before night fell. I awoke again and I lay on my bed, looking out the cracks into the darkness. I wondered where my regiment was. Was Valentina alive? I hadn't seen her in the compound, so maybe she hadn't been caught. She could be back with the 46th already. Did they think me dead? The last time Valentina had seen our aircraft, it was in flames and heading for the ground.

I hoped they thought I was dead. Better than knowing I was a prisoner of war. I knew my friends; they wouldn't sleep, knowing I was alive like this. They'd be tormented and heartbroken as I'd have been if they'd been in my place. For a fraction of a second, I started to wish one of them was here instead of me, but the thought was so disgusting I wanted to drown in my shame. Maybe I deserved this, for being such a bad friend and horrible human being. What had I ever done for them, while they had always been there for me? When I got back to them, I swore I'd be a better person; a better friend.

Had they moved bases yet? Were they targeting the men who had caught me? I hoped so. Maybe they'd bomb near the compound, or here. My blood ran cold at the idea; our efficient regiment and bombs, against which this tiny wooden hut wouldn't stand a chance. Better they kill me than the Germans, but I would still rather escape than die.

I was still thinking when dawn and the guards came. One pulled me up, bringing tears to my eyes as his fingers dug into my injured arm. They had no regard at all for my wounds, and neither spoke as they led me to a small office.

Two officers of the Luftwaffe, the German Air Force, sat behind a desk, opposite a single chair.

Obscurely, it reminded me of my interview in Moscow, so many years earlier. This time though, there was no charismatic Marina Raskova to remind me of the perils of war. The speech she gave one day at Engels came back to me. Your examination will be on the field of battle. I wonder if this meant I had failed. For once, I was glad she couldn't see me. She would have been disappointed. I was ashamed.

"Sit, sit," one of them said in Russian. He had a round face and small, piggy eyes that looked at me with great curiosity, something that unnerved me.

I wanted to defy him, but I would have shamed myself further by collapsing in pain. I lowered myself onto the chair with as much dignity as I could muster. Luckily my behind was one of the few parts of me that didn't hurt. Sitting was a struggle; I was light-headed and in such discomfort. I had to grit my teeth to keep from groaning.

"So, you are a fellow aviator," Piggy-eyes said, sounding congenial, almost friendly. "So are we. Just by accident of birth, you are there and we are here." He nodded to the other man, a tall, younger man with an aquiline face. He might have been handsome had he not been my enemy.

"Yes," Tall-man agreed. "We could have served on the same planes, or in the same regiment."

It was absurd. For one thing, I was on the opposite side of the desk. For another, unless they were ugly women with stubble on their chins, then they would not have served with me. Did they really think that by finding common ground, I'd be more helpful?

"What is your name?" Piggy-eyes had a pen in his piggy fist, ready to take down any information I gave. He'd be disappointed.

I raised my chin and kept my mouth closed.

"Which regiment are you with?"

How has this man learnt such good Russian? Probably from interrogating thousands of us. Again, I said nothing.

"Fine, perhaps something else to start off with? Uh…why are you flying? Are your…people so short of aviators?"

I caught his hesitation in referring to us as people. If I were fit, I'd vault over the desk, grab his pen and stab him in the neck with it. It might be the last thing I did, but it would be worth it. I could see the vein, right there, pumping through his neck. My hand twitched, but I kept it still, my lips pressed firmly together.

Tall-man decided to try. "You know, we only want a bit of information. If you tell us a few things, we might find a way to return you to your regiment."

It couldn't help my eyebrows rising. Did he really think I was that stupid? They were not going to let me go back and continue killing their countrymen. I wouldn't have released me if I were them. Nor would I have released them if I had taken them prisoner.

Evidently, my change of expression encouraged them to think I was going to cooperate.

"What kind of aircraft do you fly? Were you a pilot? A gunner?" Apparently they found the idea of the latter to be amusing. Evidently they hadn't encountered any of the women snipers in the army. I remembered the girl I had worked beside outside Moscow who had wanted to be a sniper. I never knew her name; I wondered if she'd achieved her goal.

Tall-man sighed. "Perhaps we can trade? I see you're injured. Maybe if you give us your name, we'll let you see the doctor and get treated."

That was tempting. Washing my burns, some bandages and, most of all, some morphine would go along way to easing the pain. And for what, just my name? What good would knowing that do anyway?

I pressed my lips together, but then loosened them and ground out, "Nadia Valinsky."

"Good, good," Piggy-eyes wrote on his sheet of paper. "Now, your regiment?"

"We had a deal," I growled.

Tall-man laughed. "Such a wildcat, eh? We'll help you, but we want more."

They got no more. I pressed my lips harder together and stared at the wall behind their heads. I got nothing, either. After a couple of hours, they gave up and I was taken back to my solitary room and locked in. No doctor, no bandages. Not even a vial of morphine.

I lay back down on my bed and stared at the low ceiling. No wonder people gave up. The Germans were relentless and merciless. I wanted to scream out loud from sheer agony and frustration. I bit my lip — hard enough to draw blood — to keep from crying out. I would die here, I knew that now. No one could bear such pain indefinitely and not let it swallow them whole.

I tried to focus on something else, thinking back to the questions my interrogators had asked. They seemed curious that a woman would fight. They asked me about our command structure and how we'd chosen our target. Who was getting intelligence on their movements and who decided what we acted upon? How many women were in my regiment? Did we have any men?

I couldn't see how the answers to any of their questions would help them to win the war. In fact, I wondered why they were curious at all, surely they had already been told answers from other airmen and airwomen they'd captured, or from their own intelligence. Perhaps they were like those people who studied the behaviour of animals. Maybe in understanding us, they could better control and defeat us. I was not going to help them to do either of those things.

It did occur to me that by not speaking, even with all of their cajoling, I was telling them something about the persistence of the women in my regiment. That couldn't be helped though. I wasn't going to feed them the information they needed to kill my sisters. I could try to feed them false information, but it would be more difficult to keep lies straight than it would be to keep silent.

That's what I would do, I swore to myself. If they came for me tomorrow, I wouldn't say a single word. I'd sit with my hands in my lap, endure the pain and stare at the wall. There had been a knot in the timber; I would focus on that. I would let my mind wander, even surrender to the pain, but I would not speak. If they beat me, threatened me or held a gun to my head, I wouldn't waver. I would keep my sister's secrets even it meant taking them to the grave. Better that than betraying them.

Even if they let me see a doctor, I would tell them nothing. I broke down at the idea of being without pain, even for a little while. I turned my face to muffle my sobs and wept into the hard mattress.

CHAPTER 36

The officers interrogated me daily for two weeks. For hours every day, we'd go through the same routine. They would ask questions, threaten, bribe or cajole and I would say nothing. I waited for the day they would break and beat me, but they never did. Eventually, they saw the futility in the whole exercise and they left me in my solitary room, day after day, with a guard leaving a meagre meal three times a day.

As the days wore on, I became more and more despondent. The walls seemed to close in on me, pressing in and suffocating me. The days became a blur of pain that gradually worsened, so I knew my burns were festering. They smelled bad; worse than the rest of me. My skin felt caked with filth and mud. I wanted a bath almost as much as I wanted morphine.

But most of all, I wanted to leave. Even if that meant dying.

That was the only way I'd be free of the torment. If the guards had taken me out and beaten me, it wouldn't have been as effective a torture as this. Whether they intended to make me suffer or had stopped bothering with me, the result was the same.

In a lucid moment, I looked around the tiny room for something to cut my wrists or hang myself with, but there was nothing. I cried then, bitter tears, and wished I'd died when my plane had crashed. I envied all of my sisters who had died quickly, incinerated in their aircraft.

The lucid moments became few and farther between, until the day the guards came for me. They dragged me out of the room and dumped me in a hut with a dozen other prisoners. There was no explanation for the move; they just shoved me onto the floor and left me there.

I managed to crawl into a corner and curl up, my burns uppermost so I was lying on my uninjured side. Perhaps there was worse torture than being alone, for now a room full of people could see the shame of the tattered version of myself

I had become. I felt someone walk over to me and crouch down, but I ignored them until I heard my name.

"Nadia?"

I glanced up and froze. For a moment I forgot the pain, as I stared into the warmest brown eyes I had ever seen. I wouldn't have recognised him, but I could never forget those eyes.

"Nikolai?" It had been so long since I had heard my own voice I almost didn't realise I'd spoken. It was really little more then a croak and it hurt my throat.

He recoiled a little and stared as though he'd seen a ghost.

"Nadia?" he said again. He frowned. I could see him trying to reconcile the thin, half-broken woman lying before him with the girl at Engels who had boy-short hair and a ready smile.

"Yes, it's me." I felt his hand take one of mine. They felt like twigs, so frail and small. He pulled his hands back and for a moment I thought he was going to walk away. Instead, he put his slim arms around me, leaning over me and rocking lightly like a child.

"Nadia, Nadia, what are you doing here?"

"The same as you." I remembered seeing a scarecrow in a field once. He reminded me of that, a shell of the beautiful young man he'd been.

"How did you get here?" I asked, my heart wanting to break.

He lifted his head so I could see in his eyes a different kind of pain and the same shame as I had; the desire to die because living had become unbearable.

In a halting voice, stopping occasionally as his mind wandered and obviously excluding the bits too horrific to tell, he told me the story of his last, long year…

"I was in an air battle. We were outnumbered from the beginning. They should have ordered a retreat, but they didn't. Besides, we wanted to take as many of them with us as we possibly could. I shot down a Messerschmitt, but then several of their aircraft turned on me.

"My plane was damaged, but I knew I could land it. It was rough, but I made it into a field. My gunner had bailed out already, so I got out of the plane and ran. I made it to the trees and hid, but I was right behind enemy lines. They were everywhere. I would walk for an hour and then spend several hiding from patrols and troops moving from one place to another.

"And then it started to rain. It rained for two days. I was slogging through mud up to my knees. I came upon a patrol but I couldn't run, the ground was too soft and I was too waterlogged. They took my pistol and marched me back to their encampment.

"I spent a week there, behind barbed wire, with fifty other men. Half of them were so badly wounded they spent the days and nights moaning and begging someone to kill them, or calling for their mothers."

Nikolai paused to give a shuddering breath. I thought he'd said enough when he resumed speaking.

"They'd be alive when we went to sleep at night and in the morning they'd be dead. The Germans just left their bodies lying on the ground where they had fallen. We moved them over to one side, but they'd rot and flies would gather on them... The smell was horrific. It drew insects and wolves. The Germans shot them and threw their bodies into the yard with us. I thought I'd die too, but somehow I didn't."

I could see on his face that he'd hoped he'd die there. I couldn't be ashamed of him. This hell they call war is nothing like the patriotic propaganda told us. We don't just kill or die; we're destroyed from the inside, hardened like glass in the heat of a forge, made brittle in ways I'd never thought possible. The heat of battle never seemed so appropriate.

I squeezed his hand as he continued.

"They loaded the living ones onto the back of a truck and took us to a camp. I don't know where; somewhere near a train station. They wanted to discourage our army from attacking it, using us as human shields so they could bring in provisions and more men. It was so close to the front I could hear our people calling to each other, the sound of their gunfire. I thought I'd go crazy, being so close but so far from freedom. That was the worse torture I could ever imagine. That and not knowing what you'd think. I hated that you must think I was dead, but I hated the idea you'd know I was a prisoner and living like this."

He looked suddenly distressed, as if seeing me for the first time. He looked ashamed. I gave him a small smile. It felt strange to do it, as though the muscles in my face had forgotten how.

"I live like this too," I reminded him. For weeks we'd been close to each other and we'd never known it, until now. I was glad now I hadn't succumbed to screaming from the pain. He might have heard me.

He gave a sob and turned his face away. For a long time he was silent, but then he went on speaking. Maybe telling his story would help him to heal a little.

"They moved us around a lot, keeping us clear of our people. Every night, someone would die. Every morning they'd make us dig graves and throw the people in. Then they brought me here."

I waited, but that was it. His harrowing existence for the whole year. My heart wanted to break for him, although a part of me was struggling to remember him as the boy on the train and the way he'd kissed my cheek. We'd been children then, so long ago.

"One thing kept me going though," he added softly. "You. You and your letters. I didn't have them with me, but I'd read them so many times I had them in my memory." He pointed to his forehead, his bony finger trembling.

The smile I gave him was a little bigger now, although it faded away quickly. There was a flash of the old Kolya, the man who had hung on to hope that some day he'd be free. The war went on, but we had a minor victory between us.

EPILOGUE

I looked over at the American who had come to interview me. Who would have thought the day would come when an American would want to come to my small house in Moscow? For so long after the war, both of our countries had been so suspicious of each other. But times change.

I took a long, slow breath and continued.

"I don't know how long we lay there for, but I slowly became aware of the profound silence. The guns had been getting closer for days, but now they didn't make a sound. I hadn't even dared to hope our side might have won. All I hoped for was that someone would end this, and soon. A bullet in my head, a knife to my heart, hands around my throat. I didn't care, but dying slowly was too horrific to imagine. Maybe somehow Nikolai and I could...

The door swung open and I looked over, relief at the sight of guns. Finally, they had come for us. They had come to end our suffering. I screwed my eyes shut, awaiting the shot, disappointed that I was a coward after all, for I couldn't bear to watch them raise their guns toward me.

I heard Kolya sob and he lowered his forehead to mine.

"It's over, we're free," he said.

It took a full minute for his words to register. The infantry — their weapons, their uniforms — were ours.

I let out a sob of relief. If I died now, I would die in the arms of my people and not the hands of my enemy. Somewhere, very deep down was the germ of understanding. We were free. We could go home, we could live our lives; we didn't need to die.

"Can you walk?" Nikolai pushed himself to his knees and held out his hand.

No, but I did anyway. They weren't carrying a Night Witch out of here, while I had the determination to move under my own power.

I gave him my hand and staggered to my feet. I had to lean against him, but I walked out of that hut, one slow step at a time. The sunlight was a brilliant glare after months of darkness. I had to squint, but I wanted to drink in the sight of our troops, tanks and several armoured trucks. It was the sweetest sight I had ever seen.

I heard a shout and what looked like an entire division headed past the camp and along the road. Someone tossed weapons to any POW strong enough to hold one and gestured for them to follow. Some of the prisoners had been new arrivals and were still able to fight. My heart swelled with pride as they went after their captors. I envied their energy and their chance for revenge, but I could barely support my own weight. This was one fight I had to accept wouldn't be mine.

For us, trucks arrived and one by one we climbed onto the back. I was weary and thin, but I wanted to find my regiment, to let them know I was alive. We weren't given that choice though, and Nikolai needed me. After so long as a prisoner of war, he was weak and heart-sore. For once, I didn't complain when the truck left the camp and headed for a field hospital at the rear.

The war was all but over and we had survived it.

"And after the war?" she prompted me. "What happened then?"

"Oh," I said. "I'll leave the story there if you want a happy ending, but the truth isn't so happy. After the hospital, neither Kolya nor I were allowed to return to our regiments. They held us in a building here in Moscow and interrogated us both, separately of course. They assumed that because we hadn't died, we must have been in league with the Germans.

Who keeps their allies locked away and starves and beats them? I don't know, and I told them that. I told them my regiment and General Vershinin himself could vouch for my good character. And he did. They let us both go after a week, but discharged us on medical grounds. The war was over by then anyway. There was no regiment for me to go back to. The 46th was the only women's regiment to serve in Berlin itself, and I had missed it."

I had scowled at the time, but it is so long ago now.

"In 1945, President Kalinin talked to a group of my sisters and told them, 'Don't give yourself airs' and to 'let others talk about our deeds'. In other words, they didn't want us talking about being in combat. It was as though they were ashamed of us. Thirty-one women from my regiment died during the war and twenty-four earned the Hero of the Soviet Union medal. More than any other women's regiment, and they wanted us to forget and move on?" I shook my head.

"Valentina survived," I went on. It was getting more difficult to keep my thoughts in a straight line these days, so I just said what came to me. "She married a male aviator and worked in the office at his airfield. She and Sophia never gave up hope of seeing me alive again. They found Lillya Litviak's plane in 1979, so she was officially listed as killed in action. Sophia married an engineer and they both worked in a factory making aircraft.

"I saw them several months after the war ended, when Kolya and I got married. We kept in touch for many years and saw each other once a year, when finances allowed for it. All of us women, who trained at Engels and served together, meet up when we can. It's like we're young women all over again."

I got to my feet and walked to the fireplace. Across the mantel were photos of Nikolai and I on our wedding day, surrounded by our former regiments, those who could make it; those who had lived to see the end of the war.

"These are my sons," I pointed to two pictures of chubby, dark haired babies. The American woman stood up to take a closer look.

"That one has such warm brown eyes," she said, pointing.

"Alexei has eyes like his father. Mikhail looks more like me. They're grown now. Those are my granddaughters." I smiled fondly at the photos of four girls dressed in modern clothing.

"I never found my parents, or my missing brother," I said sadly. "When I came back to Moscow, there was nothing left, no sign of where they might have gone. There are graves outside the city. I suppose they must be in one of those."

"And Nikolai?" The American prompted. "What about Kolya?"

"Kolya never really recovered from his time as a prisoner." I shuffled back to my chair and sat down carefully. "He would go for days without talking and he'd have these trembling fits. We never talked about the war. If anyone mentioned it, he'd walk away. If they talked about it on television, he'd switch it off. He became a teacher, too. He taught mathematics at the same school I worked at. He was a smart man, but so changed, so broken."

I exhaled sadly. "He died of a heart attack in 1993. The Nazis broke his heart and I could never mend it. I knew he loved me in his way and I knew he needed me, but we never discussed our feelings once we left the camp. We just agreed to get married because it seemed like the right thing to do. Perhaps we just wanted some peace and happiness after all."

"And you, did you find happiness?"

I hesitated. "I found some happiness, in my work and in my children. But some days I sit on my chair at the window and think back to those exhausting, glorious days during the war, when I flew and fought and was proud to be one of Marina Raskova's girls."